# FEEL THAT

## *Life of a Child of a Heroin Addict*

By

R. E. James

FeelThaT Publishing

FeelThaT Publishing
2226 MacArthur Blvd #2736
Oakland, CA 94602
1-800-220-9571

ISBN: 13: 978-0-9997218-2-7
ISBN: 10: 09997218-2-8

Library of Congress Control Number: 2018900820

Book Cover Model Contact Information: Xavier D. Finney – Instagram @xinspace3005.
Book Cover Model Contact Information: R. E. James @feelthatvisionllc@gmail.com, and or Joscelyn Gaphardt Joscelynwiley@hotmail.com.
Book Cover Design and Photography: Justin Casanova www.justincasanova.com
Editor: Elizabeth McKague

THE PUBLISHER IS NOT RESPONSIBLE FOR WEBSITES (OR THEIR CONTENT) THAT ARE NOT OWNED BY THE PUBLISHER.

**DISCLAIMER: ANY SIMILARITY TO REAL PERSONS, LIVING OR DEAD IS COINCIDENTAL AND NOT INTENDED BY THE AUTHOR.**

### References

*The Holy Bible NKJ*, (2016). Grand Rapids, Michigan: Zondervan
Mahatma Gandhi, Moving Words. (1999). *BBC Learning inspiring language learners for 70 years.*

PRINTED IN THE UNITED STATES OF AMERICA

# BOOK CHAPTERS

# DISCLAIMER

The people referred to in this book as my "Mother, Father, Sister, are not in fact anyway related to me or my family. While based on true events, these may not coincide with what others depicted in the story experienced or remembered. Therefore, in the interest of protecting privacy, I have changed relationships, names, cities, states, and other locations. Any resemblance to actual persons living or dead, events, or locales is entirely coincidental. Some dramatic enhancements might occur to better illustrate the environment and the affects these events had on the lives of those involved.

# Introduction

While growing up in the projects, I abandoned any feelings that I had for family members who had wounded me severely or negatively impacted me throughout my life. The things that were supposed to matter—such as protecting and providing for your children—really didn't matter in our household.

So, what was I supposed to feel? Was I supposed to feel despair when my cold-hearted mother demanded that her son tie a telephone cord around her arm, so she could inject heroin? Was I supposed feel the agony of her eleven-year-old daughter's screaming in protest and pain because her mother made her sleep with adults, so she could get high?

I had to become numb; otherwise I don't know how I could deal with day-to-day pain and abuse of my own reality. You can't imagine the hatred and despair we felt for family, world, and God. And the worst part was—there seemed at that time to be absolutely no escape.

What a wonderful feeling it is when you know that you don't have any control over what's going on in your house—especially when you know the difference between right and wrong, and the difference between consensual sex and rape. In our home, what was normally right was wrong, and the wrong thing to do was considered right. It was an upside-down existence where morality was a concept yet to be invented.

I didn't know how else to deal with watching someone die violently after injecting a syringe full of battery acid into his arm. Regardless of how hard I tried to erase it from my memory, I can still hear him screaming, begging for mercy, desperate to live. Yet I wanted to live too, I needed to live, so I endured and sacrificed, and yes, I suffered. I had no choice and suicide was not an option.

Suicide is no longer a choice because everyone who attempts to commit suicide isn't necessarily successful at it-- and then the family must deal with the aftermath of that failed suicide attempt by providing them with the care that they now, so desperately need.

We had to accept our reality, which entailed living in fear, hopelessness, despondency, misery, and regret. Most of all, we felt unwanted and unloved. The Bible states, "For whatsoever a man sows, that shall he also reap" (Gal. 6:7 New King James Version). Did I sow evil that I was unaware of when I was an innocent child? If I did, I was unaware of it and yet wondered why I was reaping such a vile harvest.

Feel this? Every time I had blood drawn, the doctors had to give me a sedative and lie me down because I had a phobia of needles. My wife holds my hands as if I'm an infant and instructs me on slow breathing techniques while I count backwards from twenty as she lovingly whispers, "The doctor is here to help you, not hurt you," and then it's over.

But regardless of how hard I try to erase those painful memories from my mind, I vividly remember every scene: wrapping that telephone cord around my mother's arm while black-tar heroin rushed through her veins; her bodily fluids trickling down from between her legs while her eyes rolled back in her head because she was transported into ecstasy by the pleasure of that drug; and my mother selling my sister to drug dealers and users because she had run out of money and wanted to get high.

When that happened, I buried my head beneath the pillows and blankets, but that didn't prevent me from hearing my sister screaming, "Help me! Help me! Ron, help me!" repeatedly. The thumping of the headboard hitting the wall was so loud it could even be heard outside.

Those demented pedophiles and rapists didn't have any sympathy, compassion, or remorse for doing such a horrific act to a little girl. They repeatedly ravaged my sister, day after day, for years. They destroyed the purity of that my sister's innocence and murdered her youth!

These are some of the horrific experiences that children face because they're living with a parent or parents who are addicts, abusers, or both. Nothing is off limits; boundaries don't exist; and everything is fair game; even intentionally preparing their own children for failure.

# Chapter 1

## *Best of Friends*

It was 1987 in California and my sister and I were best friends. Our mother and father were unhappily married but we were the only children in our neighborhood who were blessed to live with both parents. We didn't have everything we wanted or even the best, but my sister and I were happy.

I loved my sister, and we did everything together—from walking to school, playing together, sitting in church, or even fighting other children. I was the youngest and Tiffany was two years older than me.

My sister was a little skinny girl with great big, beautiful brown eyes. She was quiet and rather shy around other children. I admired her because she was extremely smart. She was enrolled in gifted and talented classes, where she also excelled. She could read a book once, retain the material, and then thoroughly explain what she had read. However, she lacked common sense. If she was told to boil eggs, she would put the water in the pot and place the pot on the stove, but she would also crack the eggshells and place the raw eggs in the water.

I was two years younger, and I was short for my age. Although I was cute, my personality differed from Tiffany's. I was the outgoing type, a risk taker, and an underachiever in school.

We had issues in our household like every other family, but our parents never exposed us to their problems. I knew something was wrong, and I often pondered whether our parents were going to get a divorce.

I can remember when my parents had a physical fight-- I simply closed their bedroom door and told Tiffany that I would never let anyone hurt her. I told her that I would even kill if I had to for her to be safe. I never cared about myself for some unknown reason. I just loved my dad and my sister.

My father's name was William, and he was a bus driver who worked overtime regularly to support his family. He was a great father in my eyes, but a terrible husband in my mother's. Yet when he was the head of our household, we were well taken care of. When I say, "well taken care of," I mean we had water, lights, gas, and transportation. Our necessities were always met.

At that time, I believed that there weren't children anywhere who were happier than my sister and me. We didn't require anything but love, and we always felt loved. Our parents came up with other activities because we couldn't afford to go skating or to the movies, but the times we did spend together were quality times.

When I say quality time, I mean we sat around the dinner table laughing and joking with one another. We each had to go around and say two things that we liked about another person in the family, and you couldn't say the same things from the previous day. I guess that made us mindful about the most important attribute in a family—love.

Immediately after dinner, when Tiffany and Mama were doing the dishes, I would have alone time with my daddy. I would say, "It's just me and my daddy now." We would wrestle and play. Then, one day, out of nowhere, he surprisingly said, "Ron, one day you're going to have to take care of your mother and sister." After he made me promise that I would, he left the house.

My father's main flaw was infidelity. He had numerous women, and at times, his absence was felt more than his presence. Our father was six feet eight inches tall with a medium build. He was also in good health and loved to work out.

Oh, I almost forgot something important, because it's something that he never did around us, and that was drink. My father was a drunk. He was either drunk or in that state prior to being drunk, or hungover after being drunk. I can recall Mom asking him, "When are you going to stop drinking?"

He would jokingly reply, "When I pass out."

What was normal swiftly became abnormal in our household. The fighting became more frequent to the point where my sister and I knew that once he closed the bedroom door and began to drink, a fight would shortly occur, and then our mother would receive a severe beating. Unfortunately, children adapt to dysfunction, and that dysfunction becomes their new normal.

Regardless of what my father did, he could do no wrong in my eyes. Of course, like most parents, they tried to keep us from seeing the abuse, but their invisible faults were clearly seen. Although we knew what our father was doing, we never voiced our displeasure to our mother when we saw her with black eyes, or a swollen lip.

The beatings became more frequently, and we grew accustomed to his routine. Once he opened the bedroom door, we would make bets on how long it would take him before he would leave the house. We counted backwards from one hundred, and it would approximately take ninety seconds we heard the front door slam behind him.

Family time, quality time, and our happiness were slowly dwindling away because after a fight, he wouldn't return home for a couple of days. I didn't know what to say to Mama, so, majority of the times I hugged her, and told her that everything was going to be okay. She always claimed to be okay, but I knew she wasn't. *Children always know when something is wrong with their parents.* I remember being ten years old and telling my mama, "It's okay to say I'm not to be okay."

My mama, Rachel, a stay-at-home housewife, was a relatively short and heavyset woman. My mother's complexion was golden brown, and she was extremely attractive and always kept up a flawless appearance.

Our house stayed immaculate, and she respected our father even though he did not return that respect. She made us subsurface clean our room. The clothes in our dresser drawers had to be folded properly, and we couldn't have anything in between the mattress and box springs or any items under our bed.

She instilled in us a sense of responsibility—to do the things that we *had* to do first and then do the things that we *wanted* to do. She never compromised that ideology, and she refused to allow us to do the same. It was always first things first with Rachel.

At one point, after an entire week passed, my sister and I grew accustomed to our father's absence, and Mom instituted quality time in our life once again. The quality time that we spent with my mom masked my pain about feeling like the other children in my neighborhood who had absentee fathers.

Once our mother noticed that we had become used to his absence, she established a daily routine for us because she didn't want us to feel like we were abandoned. We adjusted and welcomed her routine because we were happy again. Our father's absence was compensated for by our mother's love, but that was once again short-lived because eventually our father returned home.

I was perplexed by his return. A part of me wanted my father in my life, but I wasn't ready to give up the happiness that my mother displayed. I pulled Mom to the side before she went into the bedroom and closed the door, and said, "Mom I don't want him here."

She turned around, and by the look of scorn mixed with fear on her face I thought that I would get punched, slapped, or beat with The Brown Extension Cord, but she said, "One day, you're going to have to love and forgive a family member who has done you terribly wrong." Then she followed her husband into the bedroom and closed the door.

My sister and I looked at one another in silence, but our silence spoke volumes to one another. I sat on the bed and tears welled up in my eyes while she stood in front of the clock, but this time, she didn't count backward. I immediately asked her, "What are you doing?" but she didn't reply. "Tiffany, what are you doing?"

Then we heard a loud sound as if something heavy had hit the floor. Then I heard my mother scream, "No! Lord, NO!" I was looking at Tiffany, and her eyes were telling me to go and check it out, but I was afraid I'd see my mother lying on the floor after being thrown there violently by her husband.

My heart was racing, and I was shaking. I tried to move but I couldn't. Perhaps I was in shock. I felt warm urine start to run down my right leg, but I was still in control enough to stop it. I heard Tiffany say, "Ron, you're peeing on yourself!" and then that's when I came back to myself. I started to walk into the bathroom, but I stopped because the bathroom was the only room that separated both bedrooms.

"It's okay, Ron. Clean yourself up before Mama comes out here and whips you," Tiffany said.

I reluctantly walked into the bathroom, grabbed a towel, and quickly washed myself up while my sister cleaned up the mess that I had made on the carpet. When I was changing clothes, I heard my mother's voice. "Are you almost done in the bathroom?"

"Yes, I had an accident," I stated. As soon I exited the bathroom, my parents' door opened, and from the look on their faces, I believed in my heart that they were going to tell us that they were going to get a divorce. They were both so serious and we learned later that Mama had fallen onto the floor from shock rather than being pushed.

"Go into the living room," my mother said. We sat down, and before my mother could begin to speak, my father interrupted her.

"Yawl know that I would do anything for my family. I've driven that cab all day and half the night at times to provide for our family. I've made many mistakes, but first and foremost, I'm asking you all to forgive me for being absent. I've made many mistakes, and it's time for me to shed light on this darkness. I've had an affair on your mother. Yawl have a sister. Her name is Susan, and she's two years old. I've asked your mother for forgiveness, and now I'm asking my children to forgive their father. I hope you're able to do that."

He looked at us intently for a moment to make sure we had understood what he was telling us then continued, "On another note, I want you to use your time wisely. The time that God grants us on earth should never be taken for granted. You will never know how much time you have until one day, you run out of time. Do you know what I'm saying?"

"Yes," we replied.

"I love you, and regardless of how much I wish that things were different, unfortunately they're not. Son, a man takes full responsibility for his actions even if he must suffer the consequences. Because of my drinking, I'm sick, and I'm dying. I used to jokingly say, 'I'll quit when I pass out,' and now I regretfully say, 'I wish I had known back then what I know now because I would have probably stopped drinking.'"

My father paused for a minute, his brow crinkled, and his eyes seemed to moisten before he said, "I have cirrhosis of the liver."

"What's that?" I asked.

"My liver is damaged due to my drinking. The doctor said I'm dying, but God has the final say. I have an appointment in a couple of days, and I will tell you exactly what the doctor said. I promise I will no longer conceal things from my family. I'm sorry. I'm truly sorry. There comes a time when you have to make it right because there might not be another opportunity to."

Mom was crying as they exited the room, and I didn't have any comforting words for my sister. Sometimes when you don't have anything to say, all you can do is what I did, and that was to hug Tiffany tightly. We both cried. Nevertheless, I wanted her to know that I would always take care of her.

My father doctor's appointment was approaching, and the presence of life that once resided here suddenly seemed nothing more than a waiting room for death. The sound of laughter that occupied our dwelling was exchanged for the silent footsteps of the dead walking throughout the house.

The hate I had for my father turned into fear, and fear was replaced with unconditional love because I didn't want my father to die. "What would become of us when our father died?" I thought.

I promised my sister that I would take care of her, but I didn't have a clue about what to do. I seriously wondered whether it was possible for a child to properly take care of another child.

Inappropriately, in far too many households, the parents and their children switch roles. The children assume the responsibility of the parents because of the parents' inability to take care of their own children—either because they're severely depressed or they're afflicted with substance abuse.

Not only does the child have to take care of their siblings, they also must care for the parents. Therefore, it does happen in an abundant number of households, but it's concealed because children are conditioned to believe whatever happens in their homes must stay in their homes.

I already had self-esteem issues because of my small stature, but what choice did I have if my father died? So, for the first time in my life, I said, "God help us all!"

The day was July 3. It had finally arrived. Mom didn't want to accompany my father to his appointment because she wanted me to go. I felt wanted, and that felt good. I kept repeating, "Just me and my daddy," like I used to after dinner when we sat on the couch. I was happy that I was going with my father, but I couldn't control my bladder because I was so nervous. We stopped several times on the way, so I could use the restroom.

Upon our arrival, I had to use the bathroom again. He instructed me to sit in the waiting area after I finished if they had already called him back to be examined. I didn't know what to expect, and after I finished, I opened the door to see my father sitting down calmly in the waiting room.

Whatever the diagnosis was, it appeared that he was confident that he would beat it. As soon as I sat down, his name was called. My peace dissipated because I found myself alone without my 'rock' beside me, and I was fearful again.

My calm and confidence returned when the nurse stated that my father wanted me back there with him. I walked with my head held high, and I knew peace because I was back beside my father.

I entered the examination room, and I instinctively knew something was wrong. The doctor asked, "Mr. James, have you stopped drinking?" but my father didn't respond. I was thinking, "Surely he's not drinking because he's sick."

"At this point, Mr. James, unless you have a liver transplant immediately, your chance of living is not good. I'm sorry. There's nothing we can do at this time," the doctor stated.

"How long do I have?"

"One, maybe two weeks at best."

"How long do I have if I don't stop drinking?"

I heard this, and I was thinking, "You're drinking knowing that you aren't supposed to drink! You don't care about us! You don't care about dying!"

"I'm sorry, Mr. James. Stopping at this point might give you a few extra days, but I seriously doubt it. Your liver is extremely damaged. Basically, you don't have too much of a liver left. Medically, I'm surprised that your organs haven't shut down."

I felt like I should say something, but I didn't know what to say. I was disappointed to know that he didn't care about us.

"Okay, Doc. I'll see you in two weeks," my father said.

We walked out the office, I with my head hanging down. "Pick your head up!" my father said. I took a deep breath and held my head up high because I wanted approval from my father. I was looking at him, and his eyes were bloodshot and dim. *Some lamps stop illuminating.*

Once we were back in the car, he broke down in tears. I was crying because he was crying. He hugged me tightly, and now I was crying uncontrollably. I was expecting the worst because his eyes were dimly lit, and he had that deer-in-the-headlights blank stare on his face.

On the way home, he was telling me to be strong while he was pouring a can of beer into a 7-Eleven plastic cup. How many times do parents tell their children to do something that they don't have the ability to do?

I begged him, "Daddy, please don't drink. Don't drink, please!"

"I need my medication, and if I don't take my meds, then I won't be able to endure the pain. Son, I started drinking at age *nine*, and if I stop, I would also die. Wouldn't you rather for me to die doing something that I enjoy rather than die in pain?"

"I don't know."

"You do know."

"No, I don't know. The doctor said that you have to stop drinking."

"Yes, and the doctor also said that at this point, it really doesn't matter. It's unfair for you to put this kind of pressure on me, Son. If I don't drink, I will shake, and I will be in much pain. Ron, no matter how much we try to deny reality, it doesn't change the outcome. My truth is… I'm going to die."

Then he looked at me straight in the eyes. "You're going to step up to the plate and be the man of the house. Sometimes you'll get it right, and sometimes you'll get it wrong, but you must always take care of your sister and your mother. Now promise me that!"

"I promise, Dad! I promise!"

My father gave up on living, but he refused to give up on drinking. After being an alcoholic for years, he didn't have the desire to quit. Some people are afraid of change even though it means life, but to them, to go without a bottle means death.

When he realized that he wasn't in control any longer, that was when he lost all self-control. He began to drink more and more frequently. Sometimes when you refuse to make the right decision, that decision is no longer an option for you because you're then forced to accept what has been decided for you.

My father was losing weight rapidly, and although death was approaching, his drinking was excessive. Our mother tried to prepare us for his death, but how could you prepare a child for a parent's suicide? He was killing himself, and we all knew it. Seven days after his appointment, our father died.

We knew that our father had fathered another daughter from another relationship, but he took the meaning of unfaithfulness to a new level. William was no stranger to seeking the company of many women.

For my mother to witness so many strange women crowding around his casket, crying, it must have slowly shred her heart. I couldn't imagine what she was thinking. Not being a comforter, all I could do to show sympathy and empathy was to hug her and tell her I loved her. She didn't cry anyone. She just wrapped her arms around my sister and me.

I hated my father again because Mom's body was trembling.

"Mama, are you, all right?"

"Yes, I'm fine. Everyone needed time to say good-bye to your father," she said. Her sisters knew the magnitude of his infidelity, but they didn't warn her that it was a strong possibility that there might be more women at the funeral than the ones she knew about. *Love is an action word that requires you to do something. Countless people say, "I love you" with words, but their actions prove otherwise.* I guess it's true: the person who's getting cheated on is the last one to know.

Our life spiraled out of control after our father died. Rachel never had gainful employment, so it was hard for her to find a job without any work experience. She found solace in the fact that we had his insurance policy, and plus, we would receive benefits from his Social Security check.

Mom contacted the insurance company only to be told that she wasn't the beneficiary on the policy. She asked who was, but they couldn't release that information. I can imagine how she must have felt, realizing that someone whom she loved with her whole heart never really loved her.

She went into a great depression and regardless of how hard she tried to lean on her own strength, she was unable to jump that hurdle.

"I hate him! I hate him!". I screamed.

Rachel slapped my face and said, "You respect your father! He gave your life, and at least we have his Social Security. You be grateful for that! You hear me? I better not ever hear your talking about your father like that! You got me?"

"Yes, ma'am. But Mom, look what he did to us!"

"Remember the good and let go of the bad. We all must do that. You hear me, Ron? Tiffany?"

"Yes, ma'am," we both said.

Soon my mother found out that June, the woman who gave birth to our sister, was the beneficiary. That brought some sort of peace to our family—at least it wasn't any one of those women whom he was merely sleeping with.

His main mistress, June, was very attractive and soft spoken. He must have felt obligated to provide for his other family. After our mother explained it to us, I didn't hate my father. I just hated some of the things that he did.

Because of our father's mistakes we were left to deal with the aftermath of trying to put our lives back together again. But that's when darkness overtook our family.

Mama cried herself to sleep, and she woke up crying every day. She was mentally, physically, and emotionally scarred. Because our mother was depressed, the things that she valued didn't hold value for her any longer.

She wasn't in any type of shape to take care of herself, let alone focus on maintaining a household. Our utilities were disconnected often, and during the winter months, we slept in our clothes for warmth. Grocery shopping rarely happened, so we ate at our grandparents' house.

Rachel had too many unanswered questions, so she took the road many of us do when we need to escape unending pain. Drugs provided her with the comfort that she so desperately needed. Her drug of choice was heroin—black tar, hop, boy, or whatever names you may call it. I called it DEATH because I spiritually died while trying to survive life with this heroin addict.

# Chapter 2

## *The Brown Extension Cord*

Months after our father passed, Mom was still in a depressed state, and to move forward she recognized that she needed to get out of the house. So, we started to visit Tamara, our father's sister, on a regular basis. I didn't understand why she chose to visit Tamara instead of her own side of the family or friends for support, especially when our father hadn't ever before allowed us to visit, something I didn't understand until that day our mother took us.

That day we saw that Tamara embraced every sin under the sun: drinking, gambling, and heavy drug use. We realized that Rachel's only reason for visiting was to self-medicate with heroin. Her newfound focus was to run to where the heroin was located, while she ran away from all her responsibilities and especially us. The pleasure that she momentarily received from injecting that drug would eventually lead to many seasons of pain and abuse for Tiffany and me.

I had told my sister that I would take care of her, so that is what I set out to do. Yet it is a truly a sad thing when children must take care of other children when their parents don't have the ability to because of selfishness or addiction.

I would get up earlier than usual to make us breakfast. We didn't have much food, but we became quite fond of syrup or mayonnaise sandwiches—plus, we would split a soft drink. I would add an equivalent amount of water to stretch it between us. Tiffany named the soda-and-water combination *fifty-fifty*, and she would stand over me at times to ensure I was distributing the water evenly.

After breakfast, I held her hand tightly, and we would either skip or walk to school. I trusted my sister, and she began to believe in me, even if I didn't believe in myself. Our father had passed, and Mom was severely addicted to heroin, but we were still somewhat happy because we felt secure with each other. The only person whom I loved and cared about more than myself was my sister Tiffany.

Christmas was approaching, and I didn't think that we would be getting anything this year, not like the previous years, but Mom surprised us. We didn't wake up early like most children to run to the Christmas tree and open their presents. We would always sleep in because that was better than awakening to spoons coated with black residue and ashtrays full of cigarettes butts on the coffee table.

But this time when we did wake up and come downstairs, we saw that there were two bicycles in the living room. We jumped around with excitement, eagerly looking forward to when our mother would wake up, so we could ride the bikes. But late morning turned into the afternoon, and afternoon became early evening before we heard movement in her room. When we heard her stirring, we both ran and hugged her and asked if we could ride our bikes. She let us ride them, and we stayed outside until it was dark.

One morning, Rachel allowed us to ride our bikes to school, and on the way, Tiffany made me a bet that I couldn't ride my bike with no hands. Once I did, she bet me that I couldn't ride my bike without my hands again—but this time, I had to do it with my eyes closed. In my stupidity, I tried to do that also, and I ended up getting hit by a car.

I might not have been the smartest kid, but I trusted my sister completely, and I still didn't feel like she betrayed me. I wasn't injured so I hurriedly jumped back on my bike, and we rode as fast as we could to school.

The gentleman who had hit me followed us to school and told the principal that he had hit a small child on a bike, and he described what my sister and I were wearing.

We were called to the office, and I was scared so I swore up and down that I had not been hit by a car. They called my mom, and we waited for my mom to arrive. But after some time, Mama called the school and said that she couldn't make it, but she wanted to talk to me.

"Hello, Mama! I didn't get hit by a car. I promise, Mama! I didn't!" I said. I wasn't going to tell on Tiffany because I had to protect her at all costs, even though she had placed me in harm's way. I would rather get beaten with the brown extension cord instead of her, even though that wouldn't be the only time she failed or deceived me.

When school was over, I prepared my mind and heart to cope with an extensive beating. I dreaded going home because I knew I would have to provide Mama with answers to the questions that she would have. That ride home felt never-ending.

I constantly replayed the events in my mind, wondering why my sister would do something so out of character. What could have been going through my sister's mind for her to try to purposely harm her own brother?

I walked into the house, noticing that Rachel was in her room with the door closed. Usually, she would close the door if she was entertaining guests, and this was the first time that I was happy that she was getting high.

When she finally came out of the bedroom, she didn't mention anything about the school calling or me getting hit by a car. She told us that we could go across the street and ride our bikes if we wanted to.

We grabbed the bikes and headed outside. We started playing with a couple of my sister's classmates, and shortly thereafter, they started harassing her. I speedily jumped on my bike and rode home as fast as I could and told Rachel that two boys were bothering Tiffany.

Rachel said, "Get your butt back across the street, and you better beat them both up!"

"Both! They are older and bigger than me."

"I don't give a damn! If you don't beat them up, I'm going to beat you up!"

That was all the motivation I needed to fight. I ran across the street and tried my hardest to win, but I lost. I got jumped.

I returned home, my head hanging down in fear. I didn't know what to expect—except another beating. Before I could even open the door, Rachel screamed, "Pull your pants down and lay your butt across the bed!"

I fearfully and gingerly tried to lie across the bed on my stomach, looking back at Mom with tears in my eyes, hoping to be shown grace and mercy.

"Mom, I tried. If you saw me, I really tried. I got some good licks in, Mama. I'm sorry I didn't win. I'll try again! I'll win next time. Mom, please, I will. I'll kill 'em! I promise, Mom! I will!"

My pleas fell on deaf ears, and I received a beating with her favorite item: the brown extension cord.

After she was done with me, she said, "I'm going to give you another chance. They're still across the street, and this time, you better win! You hear me? You better win!"

I tried everything. I even bit a kid, but I lost again. This time she met me as I walked up the stairs to the front porch and greeted me not with hugs or statements like "You tried," but by hitting me repeatedly in my face and neck with a wet dish towel. "Take your butt back over there and don't come back in this house if you don't win!" she exclaimed.

By this time, the boys were gone. A part of me was happy, but the other part wanted to fight again and win because I wanted approval from my mother. I knocked on the door, and Tiffany let me inside the house, and I stood in the doorway.

I told Rachel that they were gone, but she wouldn't let it go and said, "It's your fault they left, so like I said, get your butt out of my house, and take your sorry ass, and sit on the front porch. You better hope that no one do me a favor and come and get you, so I don't have to worry about another mouth to feed."

I was in shock because Rachel knew that we lived in a crime-infested neighborhood, and it was getting dark. I tried to conceal myself by taking cover behind the two chairs that were on the front porch. I couldn't sleep, so I sat there all-night crying. In the morning, Rachel opened the door and instructed me to come back inside the house, so I could get ready for school.

# Chapter 3

## *Unfaithful Spouse*

By this time, Tamara and her husband, David, had a well-known party house. Uncle David, who was a loving husband, exemplified the kind of man who was all about family. His only flaw was that he lived for his family and not for God. He took great pride in being a provider.

On the other hand, Aunt Tamara was the opposite. She was an attractive woman of medium build who treated him without respect. She didn't have gainful employment, but she was well taken care of. Whatever she wanted, Uncle David made sure to figured out how to get it for her. She had a closet full of clothes and shoes, but although Uncle David's income was adequate, other men also contributed to her high-maintenance lifestyle.

Aunt Tamara wasn't faithful to her husband, and he was aware of it. She didn't try to conceal her infidelities. She would flirt and kiss other men in front of other members of the family, including her husband. I believed that she had a sex addiction that was even greater than her drug addiction.

Uncle David was loyal and always remained faithful to his wife. He wasn't educated, but he broke his back for his family. Financially, they were doing well, but spiritually, they were lost, and either they didn't know it, or they didn't care. It's possible to be lost and not know it—just look around at so many people on earth today. Any house that's financially stable but spiritually unstable will eventually fall—and how great will that fall be is often indeterminable.

I admired my uncle, and I began to hate my aunt for what she was doing to him. Uncle David reminded me so much of my father—excluding the absence and extramarital affairs. I was so fed up with my aunt, I asked, "Why do you cheat on Uncle David? That's what Daddy used to do to Mama. That destroyed our life."

"I don't cheat," she said. "I just wrestle with my friends, and your uncle knows about it."

I knew she was lying to me. It's a shame how quickly some parents lie to their children or at least stretch the truth to protect themselves when, of course they should be protecting those who love and depend upon them.

She wasn't moaning and making strange noises just from wrestling. I recognized those sounds from an early age because Rachel and William at times would have sex with the door partially opened.

Years later, Tamara started having female problems, and those problems would eventually lead her to having a hysterectomy. That's when she switched addictions. Her sex addiction then became secondary to her drug addiction.

My uncle stood by her, and I admired him even more for doing so. It's challenging and extremely difficult to love when you know you will not be loved in returned. Yet I also believe that every time you love someone, you're risking not being loved in return.

Because of her hysterectomy, the men who used to sleep with her no longer desired to have sexual relations with her. And when the sex stopped, the frequent visits and gifts also stopped. She knew she wouldn't be able to keep her expensive and excessive lifestyle, and that's when she sank into a deep depression. Her drug usage escalated, and so did Rachel's.

Instead of letting her linger in that depressed state, Uncle David worked more hours. He was already working fifty, and at times, sixty-five, hours at the plant, but he increased his working hours to seventy hours every week for her to maintain her extravagant lifestyle.

He was paid weekly, and he signed his check over to his wife but requested two things: a fifth of Jack Daniel's liquor and a carton of Marlboro Red cigarettes. I thought that would entice her to love him, but it didn't.

During one of their parties, Tamara was bold enough to sit on another man's lap while they were playing cards. He was kissing her on the cheek right in front of Uncle David. I saw pain in his eyes, and the look he had on his face was the same look of hopelessness Mama's face displayed at our father's funeral.

So, like every other member in my family, he began to drown his problems with alcohol. The more he drank, the angrier he became. He started making rude comments about his wife's infidelities. I remember once, when he reached that drunken stage, he blurted out, "I don't know why all of these men still want to sleep with you because your stuff is colder than Frosty the Snowman."

There was silence throughout the house; even the music stopped. The visitors started to leave when he went into the bedroom. He came back out with a gun in his hand and started shooting. It was a blessing that he didn't kill anyone, but in his carelessness, he managed to shoot himself in the leg. He was rushed to the emergency room, but unfortunately, the doctors had to amputate his leg. Some choices have consequences that you are no longer in control of.

I always wondered what Tamara felt. Did she reflect on her actions and how much pain she had caused her husband over the past years? Was she remorseful? Perhaps she just didn't care. She robbed her own husband of the one thing that he valued and took pride in—that is, being a provider. But because she took his livelihood away from him, his will to live also vanished.

He didn't appear to be happy, and just like my father, there wasn't any life left in his eyes. He sat by a tree daily in his wheelchair drinking and staring at cars. I'd seen it before, and just like my father, he was drinking himself to an early grave.

The life that he once knew was gone, so he gave up on living and embraced a slow and agonizing death. *Some people don't know Jesus Christ and don't have the faith in Him they need to rely on Him to see them through rough times. They don't realize through Jesus Christ there's HOPE, not hopelessness.*

We all thought that Aunt Tamara wouldn't treat him well because they could no longer afford to live a lifestyle of frivolous spending. They succumb to their new normal and that was relying on the State for assistance. Unexpectedly, she began to display compassion, affection, and love, but it wasn't received well nor reciprocated.

We knew that Uncle David, like my father, had to either stop drinking or prepare for death. Six months after Uncle David's accident, he passed away. Unfortunately, everyone who's wounded doesn't necessarily heals or want to be healed.

# Chapter 4

## *Wanted to Be Loved*

After Uncle David's death, my mom felt remorse and she couldn't obtain the high she once received at Aunt Tamara's. That's when the place where we lived—a place we had once called home—turned into a party house. Everything that went on there was associated with that type of house like violence, alcohol, drugs, and all types of sexual immorality—including rape.

When my sister and I thought that the blackness in that type of darkness couldn't get any darker, it mentally, physically, emotionally, sexually, and violently did when our mother met Steve.

I was nine, and Tiffany was almost twelve when Steve first moved into our home. We were still mourning our father's death, and Rachel's addiction meant she eagerly welcomed a stranger into our home. I hated him because my father had told me to be the man of the house, and I knew from past experiences that Rachel would eventually love him more than me. *Some desolate homes aren't meant for dwelling because death lives there.*

So, I decided to tell lies about him, hoping that I could sabotage their relationship, and he would move out just as fast as he moved in. When Steve would leave that's when I would put my plan into action. I would immediately tell mama lies like "I caught Steve watching Tiffany bathe."

But she nonchalantly motioned me to leave the room without saying one word. That's when I knew she didn't care because her silence to spoke for her. I was heartbroken, and I never looked at my mother the same. The love I had vanished like smoke in thin air.

I cried daily. I fell asleep crying and I woke up with tears in my eyes. I knew something tragic was going to happen, but I didn't know what. I repeatedly told Tiffany, "To stay away from Steve." I didn't know why, but I intuitively knew something wasn't right with him.

Some dogs don't bark at strangers just because they're strangers. An animal will always recognize another animal, even if he's in human form. And if he's around the animal is alert and watchful of his every move. Therefore, I kept my eyes on Steve, and I studied his behaviors. I shadowed him, but never conversed with him.

One morning, I was getting a bowl of cereal and noticed that the bottom of the spoon was black. I didn't know why, so I asked Rachel.

She answered, "It's none of your business, and bring me the extension cord!"

"Am I going to get a spanking? For what? What did I do?" I frantically pleaded.

"Do what you're told!"

"Mama, please! I'm sorry! I won't do it again!"

"You know the rules!"

Before Rachel would beat me, I had to go and immerse myself in a bathtub full of water, and then I had to lie across her bed naked. My begging and beseeching fell on deaf ears, and every beating, I wondered if this would be the time she would accidentally—or intentionally—kill me.

She wasn't in control something was controlling her, nor was she in her right mind. Some entity, some sort of demonic spirit possessed her, and it ruled over her.

I's persistently beg and plead with her in the hope that she would be merciful, but mercy didn't live here. "Lie your butt down!" she'd yell, and then she'd start on her rampage.

This time the pain was unbearable—not because she beat me any differently, but because Steve was standing at the door, smiling. I refused to give him any more satisfaction by grabbing for the brown extension cord or letting him hear me wail, so I buried my face in the pillow and stopped crying. Those murderous thoughts that infiltrated my mind consoled me. "Kill Steve and your mom, and you will be free." I agreed with that **dark** voice.

Because I refused to cry, that aroused her anger even more and she put additional force behind each swing. My face tightened, and I turned my head to the side to see if Steve was still witnessing the abuse, and that's when tears uncontrollably streamed down the side of my face.

I elevated my head and noticed specks of blood on my white sheets. What I saw hurt me more than the actual pain, so I closed my eyes and placed my face back into my pillow. Once I relaxed and got accustomed to the pain again, that's when my session of punishment (for what exactly?) ended. Rachel stopped and exited the room without saying a word.

I covered myself with the blood-speckled sheets and placed my pillow in my mouth as I rocked back and forth in the fetal position, crying internally and externally at the top of my lungs.

Rachel fiercely threw open the door, and it made a loud boom as it slammed against the wall. "Stop that crying and throw those sheets away! You're a bloody mess. Get your butt back into the tub. Then you will be clean and cleansed of your wrongdoings."

Usually, after the beating and the bathing, Rachel, Steve, and Tiffany would go to the grocery store and buy snacks. They would then spread the snacks across Rachel's bed as they sat in a circle and ate them. That was the second part of my punishment, but I called it torture.

I wanted to be included, so I said, "Mama, I didn't grab the extension cord or run from you this time when you spanked me, plus I'm sorry for disappointing you because I deserved a spanking. Do you think I can have some candy too?"

"No!"

I'm mad at myself for asking. 'Why do I keep torturing myself?' I questioned. I knew I had to get used to it because it wasn't going to change.

One time, when the candy was almost gone, Mama said, "You can have some—under one condition."

I blurted out, "I'm sorry, Mama, and I promise you I will not ask any more questions."

"No, that's not the condition," she said as she walked into the kitchen.

She came back with the butcher's knife in her hand. I was crying, pleading with her. "I don't want no candy. I don't want no candy!"

"You asked for some, and you can have some if you can grab the piece of candy you desired without getting your fingers or hands cut up or cut off. It's just a game to see who's the quickest."

I feared that she might kill me if I didn't try, and I was scared that if I did try, I would lose a finger or even a hand. I was perplexed, not knowing what I should do. I decided that losing a finger or a hand would be better than losing my life. Somberly, I said, "Okay, Mama, I will play."

I quickly attempted to grab the Now and Laters candy, and she cut my knuckles.

"Ouch!" I screamed as the excruciating pain I felt caused tears to run down my face. I couldn't believe my own mother would intentionally harm me. I gathered myself to the best of my ability and decided to try again. I wanted to beat her at her own game.

I reached for the Lemonheads, got cut. Tried again, got cut. Tiffany was hysterical, begging me to stop trying, but I was determined. I had to show my mother. I tried again, got cut, again got cut, and again, and again and I got cut. 'I hate you! I hate you!' I repeated in my mind because I was too afraid to voice it aloud in fear of what she would do to me.

My hand was bleeding, but not mangled, so I was going to continue until I looked in my sister's face and noticed tears welling up in her eyes, and I heard her heart saying, "Ronald, please stop. That's enough."

*Sometimes words that are spoken through our eyes are more impactful than spoken words.* That's because those words were from her heart and soul, not just voiced words, so for my sister I stopped.

I headed back into the bathroom to examine the extent of the damage done to my hand. My sister wrapped my hands in a white towel and applied pressure to stop the bleeding. That towel also had to be thrown away.

I didn't want to live, but I was too afraid to die. 'Kill them,' that **dark** voice exclaimed. 'They don't deserve to live. That's the answer to your problems.' Violence is never the answer. "Vengeance is mine thus saith the Lord." and we all deserve to live. *Thank God for His grace and mercy.* Although I hated my life, I couldn't envision killing my own mother.

I changed my clothes, hugged my sister, and told her that I loved her, but all the while, I was thinking I could not live like this. I locked the bathroom door. I didn't know what I was going to do. That **dark** voice gave me options. 'Since you don't want to kill your mom or Steve, your only solution to your problem is for you to kill yourself. Suicide is less painful, and you can die in your sleep by overdosing on pills.' Alas, when we choose the lesser of two evils, we're still choosing evil.

I made my decision-- I was going to run away. My neighborhood wasn't the best, and for me to runaway to my grandmother's house I had to walk through a place known as Pressure Corner. The worst of the worst resided there, and everything that your flesh desired could be found there.

Pressure Corner was a dead-end corner full of abandoned and bordered up homes at night, it was pitch black because all the street lights had been shot out. People loitered in and around those houses all hours of the day, but mainly at night. Children my age and younger, visibly carried weapons. They were either lookouts or they sold drugs for the guy who ran Pressure Corner, Xavier.

Zay was a well-known killer who had a taste for luxurious things. He was respected by many but feared by all.

I gathered up enough courage to finally leave, and I climbed out our bathroom window. I ran as fast as I could because it was getting dark outside, and I knew that it was probable that I would be confronted by someone or some type of evil.

It was a long way to my grandmother's house, and I remembered that I went to school with a friend who lived at the entrance to Pressure Corner. I stopped at his house and his father answered the door and said, "Devon was not home." *Some roads are meant to be traveled alone.*

I was fearful, but not afraid enough to turn back. Fear propelled me forward. I decided to walk and not run because I didn't want anyone to know how I really felt—and that was scared. The eyes of the evil were upon me, but I didn't see anyone. Their presence and odor grew stronger therefore I stopped. But before I could turn around and visibly see what I felt, I was forcefully grabbed and lifted off my feet.

I closed my eyes in distress not knowing what the future holds for me. I decided to kick, yet in still it had a strong hold on me. I felt someone's warm breath and it appeared to be someone's tongue licking my ear. I frantically screamed and kicked, wilder and wilder until I was finally free.

I sprinted through Pressure Corner and ran without stopping to my grandmother's house. I banged on the front door and my grandfather let me in. The front of my pants was wet from urine, and I was shaking, trying to explain to them what happened. My grandmother called my mom and told her that they were taking me to the hospital.

The hospital did a complete work-up on me. They did numerous cultures on me by swabbing my mouth, rectum, and my ears. I began thinking that running away wasn't such a great idea. *We can run from problems, but problems will always find us.* They told my grandparents that they also wanted to test my blood, but I had a phobia of needles from watching Rachel shoot heroin.

I'm at the hospital pondering upon the events that had transpired. Rachel had beaten me bloody, my hands were cut up, I'd been sexually assaulted, and now they wanted to take blood which I hated more than everything. I didn't think that I could endure too much more before I took my own life. I asked God why, but He didn't answer—or at least I didn't hear Him. I missed a couple of days of school, and then my grandparents took me back to Rachel's house.

Even though Tiffany could do no wrong in my eyes, I began to hate girls and women because I associated them all with Aunt Tamara or Rachel. There was an older girl who attended Belmont Elementary School with me her name was Brandi. She persistently asked me if I wanted to have sex with her. I was only--- years old.

She must have been abused or molested when she was younger because she was already aware of sex when we were only in the fourth grade. I liked her, and I knew that she liked me, but I didn't know anything about sex. I'd heard what I thought were sounds of someone who were having sex from my mother's room, but what she was doing to make those sounds, I didn't know.

I thought about what Brandi was constantly asking me, and one day at lunchtime, I decided to give it a try. She escorted me to the front of the school where there were some large bushes where children hid and smoke cigarettes.

She started touching me and then pulled her pants down. She unzipped my pants and began to pull mines down. My eyes were wide because I'd never seen a naked girl before. I didn't know what to do. I had a number-two pencil in my hand and I began to thrust it inside of her. I didn't know why, but I couldn't stop myself. She ran off screaming, trying to pull up her pants while streaks of blood ran down her legs.

The principal called the police, and a few days later, the school expelled me. Luckily, my grandparents were rich enough to protect me because I didn't go to jail. The police spoke with my mother, and I had to undergo a psychiatric exam to determine if I was mentally stable.

My grandmother took me to a psychiatrist she personally knew, but that didn't help me at all. It protected me, but the help I so desperately needed I never got. I couldn't tell anyone what I was going through because if I did, Rachel would kill me. I said the right words, but I didn't believe I was stable. I was traumatized, and it was only a matter of time before I did the unimaginable.

On the day I was finally able to attend school again the weather was horrible. Rachel said that we didn't have to go because we couldn't ride our bikes and she wasn't going to enjoying her company to take us.

On rainy days we would ask our neighbor Levi to take us. Levi was an elderly man who often had blackouts, nor was he a good driver. I believed he was also having sex with Rachel, and that's why he was eager to take us to school at times. After all, what else could we think when Rachel had different men coming in and going out of our home on a regular basis?

Mama said, "You don't have to go to school if you didn't want to go." Tiffany didn't want to, but I preferred to be at school rather than at home. I walked down the street and asked Levi if he could take me. He asked about Tiffany. I said. "She's not going. Just me today." He told me to wait a minute while he retrieved his keys, and then we headed to his car.

While he was warming up his car, Levi said, "I purposely set my alarm clock to make sure I'm up, just in case you need a ride to school. I know you can see me when I'm looking out the curtains while you and your sister walk to school." That made me more uncomfortable, and I wished I had stayed home like Tiffany.

The more Levi talked as he drove, the less he focused. He started weaving across the solid lines, and I politely asked him if he was okay to drive. He said "yes" and then all I remember was him swerving towards a parked car and he crashed into the car.

I was disoriented because my forehead slammed against the dashboard and it was cut open. Blood was gushing from my head, but instead of attending to my injuries, Levi was conversing with one of the witnesses. I panicked, slithered out of the car and ran off to school thinking, "Mama is going to kill me!"

They took me to the principal's office and I said, "Don't call Mama. Please don't call her. I'm going to get into trouble." They ignored my crying protest and called Mama anyway.

When Rachel picked me up from the hospital, for the first time since my father passed, she displayed genuine love. I was so thankful! I told her, "I love you, Mama," and she gave me the biggest hug I'd ever received from her.

# Chapter 5

## *Accustomed to Death*

Steve and Rachel continued dating until their drug use took them both to new downhill. They argued constantly about who was using the most dope, and when some heroin mysteriously disappeared, Steve blamed Rachel. He asked, "Where is it and I'm not going to ask you again?"

I saw real fear in Mama's eyes for the first time in my life, far more intense than the way she used to look at my father before he would hit her. She repeatedly said, "I don't know. I don't know."

Mama honestly didn't know what he was talking about because I was the one who took the balloons of heroin. I had flushed them. I thought it was the right thing to do at that time, but I wasn't sure any longer and I'm not going to admit that I took them.

Steve viciously beat Mama over forty dollars' worth of heroin. I thought that I would be happy because she was finally feeling what I'd felt

—unwarranted pain. It's one thing to get punished for being guilty but it's a different kind of pain when you're punished and you're innocent. I wanted to help her, but a part of me didn't want to.

My sister and I watched, trembling in dread as this strange man who had entered our home choked and punched our mother repetitively until she was unconscious. Once her seemingly lifeless body hit the floor, that's when Steve fled. He probably thought, like we did, that he'd killed her, and she was dead.

Tiffany grabbed some towels and applied pressure to our mother's bloody mouth and nose while I shook her, crying and saying, "Mama, wake up! Mama, wake up!"

When she awoke, we asked her if she wanted us to call an ambulance, but she adamantly declined.

The following day, her face was severely swollen. It was hard for us to eat dinner because her face was so disfigured. She didn't look the same, and nor did she act the same after the beating. She seemed to hate everyone, including Tiffany now and she was always the loved child. What have I done? I didn't know if she thought my sister had something to do with the heroin mysteriously disappearing, but she hated us equally.

My mother's younger sister found out about the fight and wanted us to move to Kansas. Gail thought that it would be a good idea for all of us to leave so Mama wouldn't encounter any more problems from Steve.

So just like that, we packed and moved. Tiffany believed that our lives would improve, but I knew that they wouldn't. *Wherever you go, your reality chases you.* Rachel was still addicted to heroin and running from problems never solved them. Eventually, I foresaw that evil would catch up to her and us. She was possessed and oppressed, therefore it could only get worse.

When we arrived in Kansas we realized that Gail partied harder than Rachel—plus to be small she was extremely violent. She carried a straight razor and was well-known for using it. Any way you looked at it-- our aunt was bad news. I was amazed to see how much hostility, anger, and hatred could dwell in this small woman.

When there was a party, violence was also present. It became our new normal. Gail would use her razor and Rachel would beat the aggressors with a hammer. After a while, I hate to admit it, but the dysfunction was entertaining. I looked forward to it.

I started participating in the festivities and grew quite fond of beating up adults because for once, I was inflicting pain instead of being afflicted by it. Mama took great pleasure and pride in my new behavior and of course, after years of desiring her approval, that enticed me to be more active in their fights.

During one party in Gail's absence there was in a drunken rage. Rachel quickly went into the bedroom and retrieved the hammer. She walked to the card table and hit the woman in the head with it. When the woman fell backward, almost falling through the glass window, Mama grabbed her and slammed her on the table.

I ran and started punching the woman in the face while Mama was hitting her with the hammer. Tiffany pitched in, throwing empty beer cans at the woman as if those empty cans would do any damage. Her cans hit us more than they hit the woman.

When Gail heard about it, she hugged and kissed me on the cheek while we laughed about the incident. This was the first time I found pleasure in causing harm to another one of God's children, but unfortunately it would be far from the last.

It was a rainy day in Kansas, and the presence of evil was prevalent in the air. I was afraid, and Tiffany and Mama also felt something was wrong, but we didn't have a clue to what it was. Mama decided not to shoot heroin and I wondered how she was going to endure the withdrawals.

I asked, "Mam what's wrong?"

She said, "I don't know, but something isn't right!"

We thought maybe Steve had found out where we lived, so she called some of her old contacts to find out. They told her Steve was still in California shooting heroin. Nevertheless, Mama told us to stay inside the house and reminded us that we better not open the door for anyone. That meant she could no longer endure the withdrawals and she dozed off for a couple of hours.

That afternoon, Gail called and asked her sister if she needed anything from the store, and Mama said, "No, but be careful."

I looked at my sister and I noticed tears had welled up in her eyes. Those tears and her expression was the same one she displayed when she asked me to stop playing the Butcher Knife game.

The phone rang and we both jumped. It startled us. It was my grandfather asking to speak to Rachel. So, when we woke our mom up and gave her the phone. Our grandfather never called. It was always our grandmother, so when he asked if we had heard from Gail, Mama started crying and asked, "What happened to her?"

"I don't know! That's why I'm calling you. I just can't get hold of her. When you hear from her, make sure you have her call me or have someone call me. Okay?" he requested.

When Gail didn't return that night, we knew something had happened. I was getting accustomed to death, so I automatically assumed the worst and understood that foreboding feeling we all had earlier in the rain. Mama did a search of the neighborhood, but no one had seen our aunt.

Three weeks later, Gail was found by the police in an abandoned house on the other side of town. She couldn't talk or walk. When the paramedics tried to stand her up, she was so scrawny and feeble that she stood on her ankles.

She was a little tiny woman, but her weight was dead weight, much heavier than it should have been. She weighed only eighty-five pounds, but it took three men to place on her on a gurney.

My grandfather Henry, who was a pastor, flew down and took her to the best physicians, but they didn't have an explanation as to why her system had shut down.

I was in disarray because I couldn't believe my badass aunt Gail, whom I admired, was stiff in a wheelchair. How could this have happened? I was mad, mostly at God because for once, although our lives were chaotic and dysfunctional, I was finally happy and had grown accustomed to the dysfunction.

Since the doctors couldn't explain what happened, my grandfather decided to take his youngest child, to my grandmother on my father's side. Her name was Mrs. Evelyn, but the family called her Mrs. Evil. Mrs. Evil, who practiced witchcraft, told Henry that she couldn't reverse the spell, but she knew someone who could. She gave him the address of a lady in Dumas, Arkansas, who could probably remove the spell.

Mama thought that was a crazy idea, and so did I. Surely my grandfather, who was a pastor, was not going to take his daughter to someone who practiced witchcraft! How does that line up with having faith in Christ Jesus or with His word? It was evident that it was a spiritual war between Good and Evil and Fear and Faith? It's easy to say that we trust God until we're faced with a real life-or-death situation. The things that we thought we would do, we don't and the things that we hate we do.

Nevertheless, my grandfather decided to go through Mrs. Evil's recommendation and take Gail to this Witch Doctor for healing by demonic and satanic rituals.

Mrs. Evil and my grandfather traveled to Arkansas to see this woman, and the Witch told them that she could reverse the curse, but Gail would die soon thereafter.

I admired my grandfather, but I was disappointed in him. How could he be a preacher and not believe in the Word that he was preaching? The same power that raised Jesus Christ from the dead dwells inside of him. Faith could heal Gail because "By His stripes we are healed" only if we believe we're healed.

The Word will only do what we believe it would do. Was my Grandfather's faith being tested? I don't know, nor will I say, but what resided in him was exposed for all to see. That entice me to wonder how many Ministers, Pastors, or Bishops don't believe or live by what they preached, probably more than we know.

Our dynamics were about to change for the worse because Rachel decided to move us back to California and bring Gail with us. Since we had resided in Gail's home, it was only right for Gail to reside with us because of her condition.

Mama didn't have a job, but at least she would be receiving some extra income for taking care of her sister. Our aunt's medical expenses were going to be paid for by our grandfather, but it took additional time to have medical care to be transferred to California.

Therefore, we stayed in Gail's home longer than we anticipated but it wasn't the same. It was our new normal, and that was the kind of normal I used to long for that I now hate.

When it was time for us to leave, we couldn't because our grandmother, Mrs. Evil, was on her deathbed dying of old age. It appeared that she instantaneously aged after they returned from Arkansas.

She wanted to speak to my grandfather in private, so I thought maybe she needed prayer, but it wasn't that at all. She told Henry that Gail practiced witchcraft with her and then began going on in depth about the activities that her and Gail had indulged in. She said, "I want to protect my great-grandchildren, Tiffany and Ron, from demonic forces and evil influences.

After she finished bearing her soul she let out a loud scream, crying, "Stop these kids from shaking my bed! Get 'em off! Get 'em off!"

Everyone in the house became frightened. Mama said, "We'd better get the hell out of here." I looked up, and the entire house emptied in a matter of minutes.

It was revealed later that my grandmother had performed abortions and sacrifices, and that she had well over fifteen abortions herself. Aunt Gail had assisted in those procedures.

I heard a voice inside me saying, "*Could you imagine seeing the very children you aborted or murdered before you die? Close your eyes and reflect on your life. Who have you murdered legally, illegally, or harmed? Do you have secrets? If so, rest assure, you and your secrets will eventually be exposed for all to see. Repent, or you will perish.*"

That voice scared me even more than Mrs. Evil!

After she passed away, we headed back to California. Rachel began to physically age from her heroin use, stress, and the frequent deaths. She couldn't be alone, so this new guy came into her life named Warren, who was also an addict. Shortly after she met him, he ended up moving into our house. Rachel claimed to love this man, but she loved any man who would get her high.

We lived in a three-bedroom home, and I shared a room with Tiffany. There were two doors on both sides of the bathroom between our room and mom's, and each could be locked. Rachel kept her youngest sister in an isolated room all by herself at the end of the house. Gail didn't have nurses looking after her like Rachel had promised. Basically, my fragile aunt Gail was neglected.

The money that my grandparents were sending Mama was being spent on alcohol and drugs. Gail was miserable, and I saw pain in her eyes. I had admired her for her strength, but I could see that she had given up, and that tore me apart.

I learned a great deal by talking to her after school, trying to get her to smile. I often wondered what she thought about or if she felt she was beyond redemption. I wondered how someone who took such pleasure in causing other people misery felt now that she's living in it. Do you really reap what you sow? Yes, I know so.

There was only one way out for her, and that was death. Although the house had multiple rooms, she never left her isolated single room, because her care was solely dependent upon addicts. Forty days after Gail arrived in California, she died in her own urine and feces.

I was frequently exposed to death and horrifying adult situations at a young age, and the pain that I hated, I welcomed because that was what was expected. I should have been careful what I asked for or welcomed because sometimes we get what we want, but we don't want what we got!

# Chapter 6

## *Pedophiles Murdered Her Youth*

The parties intensified after Gail's death. We were all lost, and that was both expected and unexpected. When a family loses three members in less than a year and a half, there's not enough time to heal, or enough time to properly grieve. Another problem was that the money that Rachel was getting for neglecting her sister vanished when she died.

My grandfather and grandmother's marriage started falling apart. They didn't talk, slept in separate rooms, and lived separate lives. They blamed each other for Gail's death. My grandmother said, "A Witch killed my baby!" but my grandfather said, "You were the one who put her out of the house, and that's when her vicious cycle surfaced."

Since the beginning of time, people have placed the blame on others instead of accepting responsibility for their own actions. When Adam and Eve sinned by eating the forbidden fruit, Adam blamed God by saying, "The woman whom You gave to be with me, she gave me of the tree, and I ate" (Gen. 3:12). And Eve said, "The serpent deceived me, and I ate" (Gen. 3:13).

It appeared that my grandparents now hated each other (and us as well) because we were attached to their own daughter.

Mama didn't have anyone else to support her habits, and that's when the fistfights began. Rachel and Warren started constantly fighting over who was doing the most dope because their tolerance level had significantly increased.

First, it was Steve, and now it was Warren brutally beating Mama! Although the people were different, their actions were the same, and therefore it ended just like before—in tears.

Our father's social security check only stretched so far because neither Rachel nor Warren were gainfully employed. What the food stamps and checks couldn't buy, Rachel had to make up for it. She decided to offer her body to strangers to get them high, and Warren agreed to it. *Love should lead you on the right roads, and what roads are right in one season could very well be wrong in the next season.*

When Rachel left the house to go on her dates, Warren purposely took off his clothes and lay in bed naked. When we had to use the bathroom, he perversely smiled at us because we weren't allowed to close the bathroom door. And from that moment on, I knew that he wanted to sleep with my sister.

I felt uncomfortable using the bathroom in my own house, so I started using the bathroom outside. I didn't understand why my sister kept going in the bathroom even if she didn't have to use it. It made me very uncomfortable and I worried for Tiffany. I tried to tell Mama what was going on, but she refused to listen.

It's impossible to make someone see something that's not in their heart to see. Denial is some people's way of accepting an embarrassing situation. Rachel's sole purpose was to get high even if it placed her own children at risk.

What some people are willing to risk doesn't necessarily line up with their willingness to be placed at risk. As long as Warren kept feeding

Mama drugs, Rachel would eventually allow Warren to have his way with my sister.

The next time Mama left the house to go on one of her dates, Warren was bold enough to ask Tiffany to bring him some aspirin from the medicine cabinet in the bathroom. I shouted, "I'll get it!" but he stated, "I told your sister to get it, so she's getting it!"

Once she brought him the aspirin, that's when he closed the door.

I sat on the bed and just waited and waited for her to come out of the room, and when she did, she had a smile on her face. My anger was provoked not only at Warren but at my sister also.

"What did he do to you? Did he touch you? Why are you smiling, and don't lie to me!" I was asking her so many questions; I was not even affording her the opportunity to answer them.

"I rubbed some Ben Gay medicine on his chest and gave him some aspirin. What's the big deal?" Tiffany said.

"I'm going to kill him," I thought to myself.

I pleaded with Rachel to put him out, but she refused to listen because heroin was her voice of reason. She truly believed that Warren was a good man. I thought if I told her that he was having sex with

Tiffany, she would get rid of him, but she responded that Tiffany has had her period and that Warren wouldn't force her to do anything that she didn't want to do. That's when it dawned on me that my own mother didn't hear anything I said. For Rachel listened only to the call of drugs, and they spoke volumes.

My last crying protest and plea came when I somberly said, "I don't want my sister to become a prostitute like you." Of course, I paid for it.

Rachel rewarded me by slapping me in the face. Then she said, "You know the drill! Get your butt in the tub, and then lie across my bed naked!"

"Mama, not again! I'm sorry! I'm sorry, mama! You're taking it wrong!" I repeated.

"Do what you're told!"

From that day on, she meant nothing to me, and I knew in my heart that I didn't mean much to her either. The sad thing about this was that I still had some hope for a normal family, like when my father was alive, but this hope had slowly been poisoned by continual disappointment.

There's never hope in man, only hope in God, and that hope does not disappoint. Most people, like those in my family, who perpetuate an abusive relationship stay in that relationship, hoping that the person they fell in love with will one day resurface, but unfortunately, most never do.

Mama started to age, and with age came insecurities. She couldn't get as many dates as she usually did, and the entire house felt the tension. She also noticed how friendly Warren and Tiffany had become, so now she started asking me questions.

I didn't know how to answer them, so I gave her the answer that she had given me, saying, "Warren is a good man. I don't believe he would force her to do anything that she didn't want to do. After all, she's growing up and having periods now." That silenced my mom.

As the months passed, heroin had taken a toll on her body and it was extremely difficult for her to get any dates. Everything that we had owned had already been sold; our television and all my mother's jewelry that my father bought her were lost to the pawnshops. So, the only thing she had left to sell was her children. Addictions can and will make people do things that they wouldn't ordinarily do. Or would they? You decide?

The first of many rapes I recall was when Rachel tried to persuade Tiffany to believe that having sex was great. She said, "The best times of my life were when I was being sexually pleasured by a man. I'm sick, and if Mommy doesn't get her medicine, she will die. You don't want my death on your conscience, do you?"

Parents who are being controlled by a demonic spirit can introduce the very thing that will eventually takes their own children's lives. Reluctantly, Tiffany agreed to be raped by a pedophile.

I was severely hurt, but my sister feared Rachel because when I told her that she didn't have to do it, she painfully said, "One of us will have to, so I'm going to do it." I didn't know what to do, so I kept pacing back and forth in my room as she gingerly walked into their bedroom.

All I recall was hearing the boom of the door closing and the click of the door locking. I stood at the door in a daze, not remembering any moans or even sounds from the headboard. I blacked out, and I started peeing in my pants, and that was the day my life changed.

The only person I loved in this world was being brutally raped and sodomized by her mother and her boyfriend. I hated everybody, including myself, because I had failed to keep my promise to my father about protecting my sister. I missed my dad dearly, and I realized that our life would have been different if our father had still been alive. I wished that I had never been born. I stood still at the door, soaked in urine, crying dry tears numb.

I came back to myself when Rachel exited the room with my sister. I remember Tiffany was wrapped in a white bloodstained sheet. I've never seen that much blood before, but unfortunately, it wouldn't be the last time.

After Rachel cleaned me up, I got in bed and placed my sheets in my mouth. I rocked back and forth, screaming internally from the depths of my soul. Although my screams went unheard by others, I could hear myself screaming very well. It was my true self. A good boy who loved his family and believed in God.

I was lost in space, wondering whether this was just a bad dream. I was present in body, but severely broken hearted in spirit. It became my way of coping. I went through the motions but remained emotionless.

What felt like a dream was my reality, and my reality had now become my nightmare. I didn't feel like eating, and I started wetting the bed from that point on.

Rachel went to the store and stole my sister some hand-me-down clothes and toys to compensate her for what she had done. I recognized what she was doing, and although I hated my mother, a part of me still loved her. I didn't receive anything, nor did I expect anything except what I'd always been given—and that was pain!

Tiffany was walking oddly, and as soon as our mother returned, Rachel placed her back into the tub because Tiffany didn't stop bleeding. I didn't know if my sister was going into shock or not, but I could her Rachel coercing her to remain calm. She even had the nerve to threaten her by saying, "What goes on in this house, stays in the house."

But in this house, there was only darkness and I didn't know how to bring in the light except to silently ask God for help and for His light to shine on Tiffany and me. Unfortunately, it didn't seem like today was that day.

Rachel went on to say that Tiffany bled more this time than her first time. After carefully examining her she noticed that she had been penetrated anally also. In fear of what she might say at school, Rachel tried to brainwash my sister by coercing her to believe that she would have died if she didn't get her medicine, I mean her heroin. Whatever last drops of love I had left, that day, were replaced with hate.

When the bleeding finally stopped, my sister only wanted to be around me. I dried my tears and I hugged her, but she didn't really want me to touch her. I didn't get mad nor did I ask her why.

She wanted to play jacks, so I sat on the floor and purposely allowed her to win every game. I didn't know how to comfort her in a delicate situation like this, but I refused to remain silent. I knew that I couldn't allow this to continue because I felt like I was letting my father down.

After months of daily rapes and sexual degradation, the bond that we shared became stretched. She thought that I was mad at her, but I wasn't. The only person I was mad at was myself.

Rachel and Warren began to fight more frequently because he didn't have the desire to sleep with her any longer. He only wanted to sleep with Tiffany. Tiffany relented, and they would have sex when Rachel left the house. I had thought that telling my mother what was going on would have made her ask Warren the pedophile to leave, but it didn't. I couldn't tell whether she was mad at me—or angry because she wasn't able to watch them have sex.

I didn't understand why a mother would want to be a voyeur by watching her own daughter sleep with her boyfriend. Was it really the drugs, or did she have a distorted mind?

I believe what was, will be again; if change doesn't take place. Therefore, once again we're faced with this same millstone of an increased tolerance level without employment. A new scheme had to be devised to support their drug habit.

Rachel taught us how to panhandle. She stole a football jersey and some awfully worn out football cleats to wear, and made Tiffany a cheerleader's uniform. Although my jersey and Tiffany's outfit didn't match, we were still forced to partake in Rachel's scheme. Rachel gave us one of those large pickle jars each, and she told us, "Say that you're raising money to purchase new uniforms before the season begins."

Since we were wearing the appropriate clothes for the deceptive roles that we were made to play, we were believable to potential donors. We rehearsed our lines, frightened of what our mother would do to us if we failed at the task at hand. Once we remembered our lines without looking nervous, she drove us to the grocery stores.

Our initial performance was at Safeway, and I was terrified. We were both in the car, begging Rachel not to make us go, but she said, "Do as you're told! You are going to do it or get a beating and then do it anyway! So, it's your choice!" Rachel had a need, and regardless how bad things were for us, her need was going to be met.

Before we got out of the car, she gave us some additional rules. There were two entrances, and Tiffany was instructed to go to one entrance, and I was instructed to go to the other entrance. "You better ask every customer entering or exiting the store. You got that?" she said in a stern, fierce tone. "I don't want any money potentially being lost because we need things for our house. Once you get a total of twenty dollars, locate me in the parking lot, and give it to me. Okay?"

"Yes, ma'am," we said.

"And if I leave, you better have your butts right there at both entrances when I return, and you better not leave with strangers, and don't let me find out you're hiding money trying to steal from me! And you better not talk to any police! You got that?"

"Yes, ma'am."

We were terrified, so we did exactly what she told us to do. Sometimes we would make well over two hundred dollars, but sad to say, it never went on things for the house. All the money we made went toward her addiction. We were puppets being manipulated by dysfunctional adults, living in fear and misery daily.

# Chapter 7

## *Help Tie the Cord*

Warren and Rachel's relationship ended abruptly, whether he got bored of her or found another addict to mooch off, I never knew. Naively, I thought things might get better now but and when he left, she started abusing me more often. I remember when Tiffany broke the dining room table; I got beat without Rachel even asking me whether I did it or not.

She stated, "I already know who was playing basketball in the house, so go ahead and run your bath water, and you know what to do!" I was looking at Tiffany, and Tiffany looked at me wondering if I would tell Rachel the truth about who broke the table. I remembered my dad's words, so I didn't say anything.

She beat me bloody and I welcomed the beating because in my heart, I knew that I was going to kill her. I refused to cry because I was numb to pain—at least, physical pain that is. The beatings with the Brown

Extension Cord intensified because of my refusal to cry. I felt like she was finding enjoyment by seeing me cry so I refused to cry.

Whatever went wrong in the home, I was the one who got in trouble. It was my fault if our lights got cut off or if the food stamps ran out, therefore I got beat. Regardless of how much I hated it, I preferred it to be me rather than my sister.

My mother was already dead to me when she found heroin. This woman was nothing more than an abuser who practiced sexual immorality. Rachel lost well over one hundred pounds and looked extremely thin and ill. When she went through withdrawals, she would state, "I need to get my sick off" and sickness to the highest degree was exactly what she displayed. Her withdrawals were so severe with the shaking and shivering that she couldn't even find an un-bruised vein to dispense the heroin through her bloodstream.

Therefore, she summoned me into the kitchen and said, "Ron, I'm sick, and I need you to help me administer my medicine."

'You mean,' I thought, 'To help you use drugs.' I feared needles because I used to look through the peephole in her room when Rachel and Steve shot dope. It made me squeamish and sick to my stomach.

I was forced to wrap the telephone cord around her arm and she injected what I called 'death' into her veins. Her eyes rolled to the back of her head and she grabbed her breast while slowly grinding her hips. Rachel's bodily fluids trickled down from between her legs because of the pleasure she received from that drug.

I was in shock by what I was witnessing and stood still in fear. I didn't know what to do, so I sprinted out of the house and paced on the front porch.

My hatred for Rachel magnified and when I helped her get her sick off I hoped she would overdose and die, but regrettably that never happened. We finally accepted our roles. I assisted Rachel in using drugs and my sister financed her addition by allowing pedophiles to kill the purity of her innocence and murder her youth!

By now, the rapes had grown so ferocious that Rachel had to hold Tiffany's hands down while men took turns having their way with my sister. I could no longer bear the pain of hearing Tiffany's screaming protests falling on deaf ears, so I walked outside.

The thumping of the headboard pounding against the wall echoed in my ear and the aggression from the pedophiles ravaging my sister invaded my thoughts. I knew my sister gave up when I didn't hear her ask for help or beg Rachel to make them stop.

I was determined to do something but did not know what I could do. I thought about going to the police, but we're taught at an early age that the Police were not our friends our enemies—besides, Rachel would probably kill us.

I wanted my mother dead but lacked the courage to carry out my plan. I had some classmates whose brothers were known killers, but I didn't know how to approach someone to ask them to commit murder for me. They used to brag about how there were so many dead bodies that they couldn't even count them all.

I figured if they got caught then I would be just as guilty as them and I would receive the same punishment as they would. But I was tired of being poor and tired of helping Rachel get her "sick off," but most of all, I was tired of hearing my sister scream because she was being sexually assaulted. I had made a promise to my father, and it was about time for me to keep it.

I asked my grandmother to start saving all her soda cans because I wanted to recycle them for money. I walked to most of the houses in our neighborhood and asked them if I could go through their trash and retrieve their discarded cans or bottles.

I would also insert small rocks into the cans and smash them down, so they would weigh more, so I'd get paid more because payment was predicated on weight. I was making nice money until the recycling center told my grandmother that they couldn't accept any more of my cans.

When she asked, "Why?" They carefully explained to her that I was stealing because I was placing small rocks in my cans. I cared only because I disappointed my grandmother, not from stealing from the recycling center. I felt like I didn't have a choice. Even when we think there isn't a choice there is a choice, it's just not a choice we're comfortable in making and that's why we say, "We didn't have a choice."

For my next venture, I asked the owner of a beauty salon if I could clean her shop. I noticed that people were more susceptible to helping children if they're honest and sincere about doing what's right.

She offered to pay me twenty dollars a week for both beauty shops. I felt like I should have been paid more because those shops were filthy, but nevertheless I persevered because I had to find my sister and I a place to live.

The money I was saving wasn't enough and moving out was taking too long. I noticed that my sister was growing too friendly with boys (or what I thought was too friendly). She started being sexually active. I didn't know why she enjoyed sex after all she had gone through, but she continued to be sexually active with boys her own age.

I didn't agree with what she was doing because she was having sex with numerous boys. Anyone who wanted to sleep with her she slept with them and I found great displeasure in that.

I told her that she had to find one boyfriend and only be with him. I preferred her to be with boys her age rather than grown men. Deep down inside I believed that if she never had been raped that her life and decision-making process would be different.

She started dating this guy name Curtis, whom she thought was attractive. He had a light complexion, and he was tall and thin. She loved him, but he was into drugs, and I didn't care for him. I never gave him a chance because I didn't want Tiffany to be with anyone. I would purposely pick fights with him, so I could beat him up.

To pay me back, evil for evil, he decided to set my sister up to be raped. Curtis told Tiffany that he needed help with his homework, and he asked her to meet him at his house after school. She eagerly agreed because she trusted him. Once she arrived at his house, there were two other boys there also. They held her arms down and gang-raped my sister.

After she had been savagely raped for hours, they allowed Tiffany to leave. She told our mother and our grandparents what happened, but our mother refused to call the police or allow her to be seen by a doctor.

My grandfather thought it would be in my best interest not to be told about the rape because they viewed my mental state as unstable. When I came home from my friend's house, I immediately asked Rachel, "Where's Tiffany?"

"Tiffany is in the after-school program for gifted and talented kids because she's smart," my mother said. I took that as another shot at me-- implying that I wasn't.

I asked if I could go over to my cousin Brian's house, and she said yes, which was strange. My cousin Brian met me halfway and then asked me how my sister was doing.

"Fine, I guess," I said.

"Fine? You haven't heard?"

"Heard what?"

"She was gang raped, and she tried to kill herself."

"What?" I started ramming his head against the side of the curb, and I left him barely conscious. I didn't accept what I was told, and I ran home. Nobody was home, so I ran to my grandmother's house. Things that were once blurry became ever so clear. Brian spoke truth.

I felt like they were trying to keep my sister away from "No, it can't be true! No, it can't be true!" as I continued to run.

I rushed into the house and was greeted by my grandfather. For the first time ever, I didn't have any words for him. "Where's Tiffany?" I screamed. He moved out of my way and told me she was in the back bedroom. They left us alone because everyone knew how I loved my sister.

I asked, "Are you okay?"

"No."

"Can I get you anything?"

"No."

"They will never hurt you again and I love you." I tried to lean down to kiss her on her forehead as she sat up in the bed. For a moment, I thought that she sat up to give me a hug, but I remembered she hated to be hugged. I asked, "What's wrong, Tiffany?"

"That's what Mama's friends used to do to me when they held me down," she shouted.

"What? What did they do to you?"

"They did that when they were having sex with me!"

"They did what? Tell me what they did! Tiffany, what happened?" My sister couldn't even look me in my face. "I'm sorry, sis. I'm sorry. I should have been there for you, Tiffany!"

"You didn't keep it! Why didn't you keep it? You didn't keep your promise. You let them hurt me! You let them hurt me!" she shouted.

"I'm sorry! I should have been there for you."

"Keep your promises and your sorry! Your promises don't mean anything to me! Why didn't you protect me? Why didn't you protect me? Tell me why!"

Tiffany began to weep, and I didn't possess the strength to hold back my tears any longer. I cried, but this time she allowed me to hug her. I'd never cried like that before in my life. That was when my transformation began.

I didn't feel sorry for myself because of my circumstances, I felt sorry for others because of my circumstances. That's when I knew I had changed and I also knew… now I could kill!

I couldn't imagine the terror she must have felt from having countless men sexually demolish and destroy her daily to pay Rachel's drug addiction. And then, when she finally finds a boy she truly likes, he does the exact thing to her that those pedophiles were doing.

She must have felt that her only escape from this nightmare would be to take her own life. Maybe I was stronger, but either way, we were two children trying to survive with every element imaginable against us!

# Chapter 8

## *I Knew I Could Kill*

Because of the habitual negativity I experienced, I turned into a monster. I vowed to my sister that this would never happen to her again and I meant to live up to that promise, even if lost my life in the process.

I said, "From this day on, I'm your mother, father, and your brother. I will provide for us, and I will find us somewhere to live." Again, I didn't know how I was going to do it, but I was determined to accomplish what I promised.

I'd tried to work at the beauty salons, sell cans and bottles, but that was a dead-end road. Now it was time for me to take this fork in the road and the only option for me was to sell drugs. After all, I've been around drugs my entire life, so it's time for me to reap the rewards instead of the misery even if the rewards were only momentarily.

That fork in the road led me right back to the place I feared: Pressure Corner! When you have nothing to lose, you're more willing to risk it all-- after all you don't have anything anyways. The place I was sexually assaulted was the very place I must return to for employment.

I took a knife with me and I was willing to kill or be killed— because either way, I would come out a winner by death, or in life. I wanted to harm someone—so at this time anyone would do and I hated my life and death might be better than living.

I saw Xavier and asked if I could talk to him.

He said, "About what?"

"Mama is making my sister sleep with grown men, so she can get high, and I want to protect my sister, so I'm respectfully asking you for a job. I'm willing to do whatever you ask, even kill if need be."

"Tomorrow, go see Christy in Linden Projects on the fifteenth floor. Ask for Christy when you reach the hallway on that floor."

I was so excited I couldn't wait for school to let out. I envisioned my sister and I were happy and safe. After school, I ran as fast as I could to Linden Projects. I reached that high-rise building and took a huge breath. I didn't have a clue to what I was getting involved in, but it couldn't be any worse than what I was already accustomed to.

I decided to take the stairs instead of the elevator. I walked up fifteen flights of stairs through the stench of urine permeating the staircase, littered with half-naked bodies of prostitutes willing to turn tricks for drugs.

I saw a trait of Rachel's character on every flight but that didn't deter me from my purpose. I reached the fifteenth floor and I asked a kid who looked younger even than me if he knew where Christy lived. He led me to apartment 1505.

I entered the apartment with the kid and he set his gun on the table. There were guns, money, and bags of balloons everywhere. One group of kids was counting money and the others were turning balloons inside out.

I was introduced to Christy, and she told me to have a seat. I'd never experienced anxiety like this before. She walked behind a sheet that separated the living room from the kitchen and I asked the kid what was behind the sheet and he replied, "Don't worry about that."

I sat on the couch eagerly waiting for my job description and then I was offered a beer. I said, "I'm only *twelve*, I don't drink," and everyone laughed at me.

She laughed and said, "My son Anthony had just turn *ten* and he drinks." I will never forget this boy's name because he was also Christy's son. After I witnessed him finishing off his beer, I asked Christy for one.

Christy came from behind the sheet and handed me a hundred-dollar bill and an ink pen. She told me that I would be turning balloons inside out.

She demonstrated how to do it, and I asked why we couldn't just place the heroin in the balloons. She said the chalk side of the balloons had to be on the outside. Customer service was first in this organization. I was being paid one hundred dollars a day for my work, and I thought that I was rich.

The next time I saw Xavier; I asked him if he could find me a place to stay. He said, "You can't stay at that apartment, but I will find you a place."

I was grateful, and I loved Xavier because my sister would finally be safe. When I told Tiffany, we were moving soon she grinned from ear to ear. I didn't tell her that I was selling drugs because of what she had experience from drugs.

I let her know that I need to know her whereabouts always and she had to continue to make straight A's in school. I would take care of the rest. I disillusioned to believe that we would be safe and I'm selling drugs!

Xavier did find us a place to live and once we moved, I felt it was time for me to kill the guys who had raped my sister. I held grudges as a kid and I had to pay them back for what they did to Tiffany.

Curtis's mother moved him to Florida after the rape. Therefore, I had to inflict harm on his parents. I poured gasoline around their home with the intention of burning his parents and younger brother alive.

I lit the fuel and the fire spread rapidly. Smoke and flames were everywhere. When I realized that they were trying to run out of the patio door, I started shooting at them with a gun I'd bought from my balloon money, but they managed to escape.

I had to leave before the emergency vehicles arrived, and unfortunately (as I thought at the time, though later I knew it was a blessing), they got away. I felt like I had failed my sister, but when Xavier heard about it, he told me that he was proud of me. He stated that he didn't think that I had that in me. Neither did I, but now I knew I could kill.

I paid the other boy who also raped my sister, Andrew's family a visit. Andrew's mother and father were divorced, and he lived with his father. Andrew also had a younger brother and sister.

I knocked on their door, and when his father answered, I tried to shoot him in the face, but the gun jammed. That gave his father the opportunity to knock the crap out of me, and he ran out of the house.

I entered the home and started hitting Andrew in the face with the side of the gun. Blood was everywhere, but this time, it wasn't my blood. I wanted to stop myself, but I couldn't.

I walked over to his sister and grabbed both of her hands and began squeezing them as hard as I could. The more she cried, the harder I tried to squeeze them. I continually squeezed her hands while I was forcefully jerking her arms like I was trying to rip them off her shoulders. I must have blacked out because I felt remorse for what I'd done to his sister later.

I didn't recall going home, but once again, when I came to myself, I was in our new apartment, lying in my bed, soaked in urine. I hated myself even more because Andrew's sister was an innocent child. I didn't know how to forgive myself because I had never been taught how to forgive. I had never been given the opportunity to forgive anyone because pain always dwelt where I resided.

I'd been taught nothing but dysfunction and so I displayed the only thing I'd learned-- and that was dysfunction. My family was afraid of me, especially my mother; they all thought that I was crazy, but I thought that I was sane. *Was it possible that I was like them?* I didn't care what people thought about me, especially the ones who never genuinely cared about me.

I was gaining respect from my co-workers and Xavier. He hugged me and called me his Savage Soldier. Xavier told me that's it a way to do things-- even commit murder. He advised me to relax and wanted me to start hanging out with James and Paul.

They were a little older than me, and one day, they wanted me to attend a school dance with them. I didn't like school dances, but I agreed to go. Then, at the last minute, I told Xavier that I was supposed to be meeting my cousin Brian because he wanted to see my new place.

Xavier told me that I could bring Brian with me to the dance. I didn't feel right about that whole day. Once again, I was there in body but absent in my mind. My body was merely going through the motions. I was sad, but I didn't have anything to be sad about. A should have known something was wrong or something was about to happen.

A quiet voice was telling me not to go to the dance, but I wanted to fit in and impress my cousin Brian. James and Paul picked us up and I still felt like we shouldn't attend, but I disregarded what I felt. *When we don't listen to our intuition we have to suffer consequences from our choices.*

Once we arrived at the dance, we all had an uneasy feeling and therefore, we decided to leave. James walked to his car to get his gun because he was sure something bad was about to transpire.

Evil has a presence and it can be felt. It was like everything was moving in slow motion. We started the car to leave and I sighed with relief. We made it. I felt relieved because I was responsible for Brian.

He wasn't raised like us. He was raised the right way—by both parents who displayed genuine love for him and one another. Brian admired me, but I wasn't anybody to be looked up to because I hated my life—and more importantly, I hated the things that I was doing.

We were driving on a four-lane highway when a car sped up and got in front of us, and then slowed down. Then another car got directly behind us. That appeared to be odd to me and then I noticed another car pulling alongside of us rolling their windows down.

I screamed "Duck!" I heard about five gunshots and we didn't get the opportunity to fire back. James tried ramming the back of the car in front of us, but he was unsuccessful.

Paul asked, "Is everybody okay?"

I thought Brian was still in distress because when we all sat up his face was still in my lap. I felt some warmness, but I thought that he was sweating profusely because he was nervous. I said, "Brian you're not my girlfriend so you need to get up," and when he didn't respond, fear set in.

"Brian, Brian, Brian, get up, man! Brian!" He didn't respond. I shook Brian and his head split open in my lap like a crushed tomato. I was trying to hold his head together, not realizing that it was too late. I started rocking back and forth, telling Brian to fight and hang on! Brian was gone, but I didn't want to accept that.

What flashed into my mind at that very moment was the last time I saw Brian was when we had that major fight. I couldn't forgive myself and

I was never the same after Brian's death. This one of the lowest points in my life.

I assumed responsibility for his death because I should have listened to that quiet voice inside me. I kept replaying what happened, over and over in my mind. We should have stayed home and now he's gone.

*Far too many innocent people die by riding with people who they don't really know or have a clue to what they're involved in. Be careful because YOU might be Brian one day!! Feel that?*

I thought that Brian's mother, Erika, was going to kill me. He was their only son. His father's heart was going to be broken. My family was going to blame me for Brian's death. I couldn't heal from Brian's death, so I took the road so many of us do, like Rachel did.

Drugs! Marijuana—Kill, Fire, Indo, Ganja, or Cush…whatever name you like to call it. I called it my stress reliever! I had a different drug of choice but the actions I began to display were the same. I was no better than Rachel.

# Chapter 9

## *Learned Behavior*

I tried hard to find out who killed my cousin. I was asking everyone. I was more focused on bringing his killers to justice—street justice, that is—than being efficient in my work for Xavier. All I wanted to do was smoke weed and locate the culprits. My work performance had plummeted, but I didn't care.

My grades were also adversely affected because for the next grading period I received four F's and three D's on my report card. I couldn't cope with the pressures of life, so I medicated myself. Xavier advised me to let it go because he would handle it, but I refused.

I wanted to kill them myself. I wanted everybody in all three cars killed. I tried to explain to him that I saw Brian's face every day. Not his natural face, but his disfigured face—how I'd seen him after the gunshot wounds as well as after our fight.

That was hard to live with, so I started sleeping with the lights on. I lived in fear from all the things that I had done. I tried to let Xavier know that it was imperative for me to find his killers, not only for revenge, but because I felt responsible for his death.

I begged and pleaded with him, but nevertheless, he sternly told me no! He said, "It's unfortunate that you had to go through so much adversity as a child, but you have to trust me. I'm looking out for your best interests. You must believe that.

Your decision-making process is cloudy, and your vision is impaired by all that weed you've been smoking. The culprits that put my son's life in harm's way will die a terrible death. I'm a firm believer in repaying evil for evil. Believe that!!"

Gandhi said, "An eye for an eye will make the whole world blind," but evil for evil is and always will be—street justice."

"Who is your son? James or Paul?" I asked.

"I'm not talking about them. I'm talking about you. You are like the son that I never had, and I love and respect you!"

I couldn't control my emotions any longer and started crying hysterically. I continued to sob like a baby and he hugged me. It had been a long time since I felt love from an adult and it felt good to know that I was genuinely loved by him.

It appeared that he cared, and I felt like I was finally worthy of being loved because my thinking was conditioned to believe that I wasn't worthy of love. It was a proper way of doing wrong and he was going to show me how to do wrong properly. *We were all lost spiritually but we didn't know it. Are you?*

I was a child living a dangerous life and Xavier wanted me safe as well as my sister. I guess he was raising me to the best of his ability. He permanently placed me on the payroll and my shift started from 3:30 p.m. to midnight. My school was out at 3:15 p.m. and I always made it to Linden Projects before 3:30 p.m.

One thing I knew about Xavier—if he expected you to be somewhere at a certain time, you had best be there by that time. He didn't tolerate excuses or tardiness. He repeatedly told us that if we were late, he'd think we were either snitching or stealing. At times, I would pull him aside and ask him if he'd found out who killed Brian and he would always say, "Don't worry about it."

I was not happy about that and I was beginning to think that he didn't care about what had happened to my cousin. I kept telling myself to trust him, but as time passed, I began to get impatient.

I was getting tired of stuffing the balloons; I wanted to do something different; something that paid more. I asked James what was going on behind the sheet a second time, and he said, "Ask Xavier."

I did, and he said, "They are the ones who make the drugs." There was where the beautiful women were located. These women were the ones who tested the product. No product would hit the street unless it was tested first to ensure that it was marketable.

After turning balloons inside out for nine months, I wanted him to promote me to the corners. He told me there was much more danger on the corners from police, other addicts, and other dope dealers battling over territories.

I knew numerous addicts because of Rachel and I believed I could handle the corners. So just like that, he gave me two hundred balloons of heroin, which had a street value of $4,000.

I hated addicts, but now I was selling the same poison that had destroyed my family and the person I treasured most, Tiffany. The first place I visited was Rachel's house. I hated my mother and a part of me wanted her dead, but I wanted to show her that I was making something out of myself. I was a successful drug dealer. *Unfortunately, some people take pride in doing bad things well. Do you?*

I left Rachel's home and headed north. The northside was nothing more than a neighborhood full of boarded houses where addicts and the homeless squatted and got high. It was one of Xavier's territories and now it was all mine. I thought that I was somebody but there was a difference between having something and being someone.

Xavier asked, "Why do you want to sell drugs in your old neighborhood?" I told him because I knew most of the addicts, but the real reason was that I was scared. I figured the people who knew me from growing up in that neighborhood would probably look out for me if I got into a dangerous situation that I couldn't handle.

Plus, I wanted to be the one whom Rachel bought heroin from to let her know that she was not in control any longer. She didn't have the power to cut my hands, beat me, or participate in sexually assaulting her own daughter. I had a pocket full of money, a pistol, and a bundle of balloons of black-tar heroin. I finally overcame pain and poverty—or so I thought.

When I first heard somebody other than Rachel say, "I need to get my sick off," I was immediately sick to my stomach. I gathered myself and I continued selling Xavier's heroin. I made almost a hundred dollars in less than two minutes. I was instantly addicted to the money.

I sat on those milk crates and gazed at my surroundings. At times, it would be painful because some of the addicts were pregnant and some would have the audacity to bring their children with them. I realized that I was part of the problem and not the solution.

I wondered what their children were going through, but I didn't care enough to stop because I justified my actions by saying "No one cared about me so why should I care about them." My sister was safe and that was all that mattered to me at this time.

I was selling an abundant amount of heroin and it became chaotic after a few hours. I had to regain control, but I didn't know how. I started cursing out customers because I was in fear.

On my first day, I sold all two hundred balloons! I was proud of myself, but Xavier wasn't. He asked me what happened out north? I didn't have a clue to what he was talking about.

He said, "There's a proper way to sell drugs." He told me I wasn't selling his dope properly. He should have realized that I was green to this type of lifestyle. If he didn't have anyone to show me then how would I know. The following day, he had his brother Bobby teach me how to sell dope.

When I asked Bobby what I'd done wrong the day before, he said, "People complained because you were demeaning them." Then Bobby elaborated by saying, "If the salesperson at Nordstrom's was disrespectful to you, would you spend your money in their store?"

"No."

He said, "Our drugs sold themselves because they were of good quality, adequate size, and provided a safe environment in which they could enjoy their high. Addicts don't want people blowing their high including their dealers." That blew my mind-- I didn't know that selling drugs could be so detailed.

I started feeling sympathy for my mother because I was the one who kept her sick. My mother's appearance and her health were declining. It became challenging to continue to sell her drugs. I wanted her healthy, but I wasn't authorized to decline a sale based on someone's appearance. All money was good money to Xavier. I had to think about the bad things Rachel had done to justify selling her drugs.

A part of me still loved what I hated. My mother also had endured a great deal at the hands of others. My father constantly cheated, and every man who had entered her life thereafter abused her mentally, emotionally, or physically. I was shown hate, and the hate always drowned out the love that I had for my mother.

One day my sister spotted our mother near the same Safeway where she had made us panhandle months back. I told Tiffany she better not say one word to her or I was going to jump on her. I ignored Rachel and threatened my sister so fiercely that she ignored her also.

My sister's eyes began to well up, but I still hated Rachel, so I stood my ground. I asked her, "Do you think I'm wrong?"

She replied, "Yes, that's our mother!"

"I don't care! She hurt us too bad! You don't understand what she did to me!"

"What did she do?"

"Nothing," I answered, and I shut down.

When we arrived at our apartment, we didn't speak to one another. I guess we were both reflecting on past and current trauma. We were safe, but neither one of us was happy. We had what we wanted, but we didn't want what we got. The bond that we once shared was now grounded in fear instead of love. She feared me, and that broke my heart.

I cried all night because I missed my old house and my mother. Neither one of us spoke, but the silence of our unspoken words spoke for us. I knew what was to come. I knew that I was losing the very thing that I loved because of unforgiveness. *Hate rooted in unforgiveness contaminate everything and everyone around you.* I was heartbroken because I sensed it would only be a matter of time before my sister moved back home with our mother.

I kept her away from the sexual abuse, but mentally and emotionally we were scarred more now than previously before. I thought that I had the mental capacity to handle the responsibility of being an adult at thirteen years old, but I couldn't. Most thirteen-year-olds can't. I guess it's true that the apple doesn't fall far from the tree because the behavior I witnessed became the behavior I displayed.

I considered myself to be a faithful employee because Xavier expected honesty and that's exactly what I gave him. I refused to steal because stealing wasn't in my heart. I didn't fear anyone not even Xavier because I was already dead inside. What he gave me to sell was exactly what I sold.

When Jimmy was caught stealing and Xavier forced him to drink two gallons of water and then instructed us to hold him down while the others repeatedly hit and stomped him in the stomach. He was vomiting water and blood.

Paul was also caught stealing and his punishment was being forced to place his head in the dresser drawer while Xavier repeatedly slammed the drawer. Consequently, these weren't the only acts of violence I witnessed.

I remembered seeing some of Zay's soldiers bring a woman who appeared to be pregnant and her little girl bound both by their hands and feet to the North.

I was surprised because I thought Xavier loved kids—one of his rules was that you never did anything to the elderly, women, or children. This girl resembled my sister who appeared to be about her same age. I pleaded with Xavier for their lives. "Please don't hurt them. Please don't hurt them. I will work extra hard to pay what they owe."

Xavier said, "I'm not going to kill them, and I'll give you my word that they won't be harmed. But this will be the only time I warn you—don't you ever interfere with my business again! You got that?"

"Yes, I do."

"In order to find somebody, sometimes you have to grab somebody." I didn't understand what he was saying, but I nodded in agreement.

He contacted her husband and persuaded him to meet him by stating he would brutally kill his wife and daughter. At first, this coward of a man stopped answering his phone, and we were in limbo, waiting, wondering what Xavier would do. Days later, the man finally decided to meet up with Xavier, and he was murdered in front of his wife and daughter.

I was horrifically upset with Xavier after that incident because I couldn't get that little girl out of my mind. I'd watched my father literally drink himself to death right before my eyes, and now, this girl witnesses her father being murdered right before her eyes. I lost respect for Xavier, and although I was getting tired of this life, this was all that I knew.

# Chapter 10

## *Killed with Acid*

I will never forget March 16, 1989. It was a sunny day in California and Xavier had James and Paul follow these two people. When I asked why, he didn't respond. He had been silent before, but this silence was different.

It was like someone was forcing him to do something that he didn't want to do. Everyone was on edge and I was extremely apprehensive even though supposedly I didn't have anything to fear.

I'd never seen Xavier like this. Something was obviously tormenting him because his eyes didn't have life in them. I knew that look well because after Gail had her accident, she lost hope, and I watched the life leave her eyes. I asked him again if something was wrong, and yet again, he ignored me.

The anxiety in my mind became my reality when Xavier answered a call from James and he said, "Bring them to Linden Projects." When they arrived, the brothers were tied up, and their hands, feet, and mouths were all duct-taped. Evidently, they had been severely beaten because there was blood on their clothing.

James took the first brother in the bathroom, took off his clothes, and shoved him into the tub. Derik and Snake entered the bathroom carrying glass jars of what appeared to be water. Derik started pouring the water on the man's genitals and that man unleashed a scream like I'd never heard before.

They grabbed the duct tape and started wrapping additional tape around his mouth and his head to minimize the screaming. I assumed that the water must be mixed with salt from the way he was screaming.

Then I walked closer, and I saw that every time they splashed his body with what I thought was water, the liquid was eating his flesh! It wasn't water! It was acid!

"Oh my God!" I said. They were throwing acid on him. I couldn't breathe, and I went into shock. I couldn't move, and I started peeing myself.

"Ron, you're peeing on yourself!" James yelled but I couldn't stop peeing.

"Get Ron out of here! Get him out!" Snake yelled. By this time, I saw Derik walking toward the helpless brother with a syringe full of acid.

My legs buckled, and when I came to, James and Paul were carrying me down the stairs. They put me down, and I was in a daze, not fully understanding what I had just witnessed. Paul asked me if I was okay, but I was unable to answer him. I wanted to go home and be with my sister, but a part of me didn't think that she wanted me around.

I was blessed that they took me home. As soon as I opened the door, I ran and hugged my sister. This time I needed to be consoled. I was crying, and now she was crying because she asked, "Did you kill our mother?"

"No," I replied, and I gave her some money and told her to go see our mother. She smiled. She couldn't believe what I had just said. I wanted her out of the house because I needed time to myself.

Here I go, placing the sheets in my mouth and screaming at the top of my lungs from the depths of my soul. I screamed until I wasn't making any more sounds. I thought that I would be better off on my own, but I wasn't. Instead of being destroyed by Rachel, I was self-destructing.

I concluded that this wasn't going to end well, and I desperately needed to change my environment. Tiffany and I were safe, but so many others were not. I believed if I branched off from Xavier, I could still sell drugs but without the violence.

Therefore, I set out to learn as much as I could about how to sell drugs. I worked harder and longer hours to show him I was dedicated. I hoped he would see my work ethic and promote me.

We had this conversation sooner than I expected, and I asked him if I could branch off and put a team together, and I told him I didn't want to sell heroin. If I sold anything other than what my mother did, I knew I wouldn't be tempted to sell her drugs.

He asked me want I wanted to sell. I told him I would prefer cocaine. So, Xavier took me to his house and introduced me to Chef Lou, a guy everyone called Low-Life. Low-Life was mixing bricks of cocaine in a mixing bowl with a dough hook. Xavier told me to sit down in the living room, and when he finished, he would teach me how to cook cocaine.

He placed two sets of rubber gloves on my hands and a dust mask over my nose and mouth. He went into intricate detail about the process of cooking cocaine. The baking soda to cocaine ratio had to be precise and he said cocaine could be overcooked.

That's when I realized I was in over my head. His only concern was the quality of the product because if the quality of the product was good, then the product would sell itself.

He also instructed me on the various methods and the different types of liquids I could use. He guided me step by step through each method, so I could grasp what method worked best for me.

After the cocaine was cooked, he let it dry in coffee filters, and then we used a dough cutter for the large orders, and a razor or a stickpin for the small orders.

The final step was accurately weighing the product. He ensured that it was slightly more than the desired weight. He said, "People love a bargain and they will always shop where their money stretches more."

I was growing up too fast and I missed what I took for granted-my childhood. I missed riding our used bikes our mother had bought us for Christmas. Regardless of how weird this sounds, I even missed getting a ride from Levi to school when it rained. The things that you take for granted will be the things you will miss severely when they're gone.

Xavier must have realized that a part of me missed being a kid, and even though our relationship was being rebuilt, I still didn't trust him, but he trusted me.

He wanted me to experience being a child again, so he asked me to take a trip with him. He took me to Disney World in Florida. We stayed in Florida for two weeks and I felt like my natural father was working through him because I felt loved.

When we returned, he decided to take the neighborhood to Astro World in Texas. This became a well-known summer festivity. The families loved him for that—plus they were his loyal customers. I never knew the magnitude of his power until then.

Basically, all he was doing was compensating families for allowing him to destroy their lives. They were letting him kill their dreams in exchange for a trip to an amusement park.

Some people are quick to say that they love you, but their heart is far from you because hatred dwells there. Xavier deceived them because he knew if he spent money on them, they would continuously spend money with him.

He threw a curve ball at the uneducated, low-income and poverty-stricken, drug-addicted individuals, and they thought that he loved them. He never trusted an addict or a drunk. He constantly instilled in us that people who loved something more than themselves, or their families couldn't be trusted.

These people didn't realize that they had paid for their own trip. But maybe he did care in his own way. *There's a little bit of good in the worst of us, and a little bit of bad in the best of us.*

He bought all the children in the neighborhood school supplies and food if they came to him in need. But once the parents stopped spending money with him, he stopped spending money on them. (Quid pro quo.)

It didn't take me a long time to be known all over town. I thought that was good, but it wasn't. It's dangerous for people to know of you, but you don't know them. That type of reputation attracted many girls who wanted to date me for what I had, not necessarily for who I was.

# Chapter 11

## *Not Far from the Tree*

In tenth grade, I finally started dating girls, but I refused to have sex with them—either because I was scared or because I had been scarred by the sexual immorality that was predominant in my household. Numerous girls wanted to have intercourse with me, but I preferred to let them please me orally. I wasn't interested in sex at that time.

I probably hated women after what Rachel had done, and you usually don't respect what you hate. Because of the lack of deference that I had, I told the girls who wanted to date me that I would date them only under one condition—that they had to sleep with my friends first.

I was deceiving them because I didn't have any intention of dating them. I was just setting them up for my friends to run trains on them.

(Trains are multiple men sleeping with one woman). Was I any different than Rachel? And I realized the irony-- that some of the behavior that I witnessed or hated, I emulated.

Often, there were seven of my friends sleeping with one girl at a time. I also remember getting upset with her after the fact because she enjoyed herself. I was worse than Rachel.

I kept the light off when I received oral sex, but I would leave the lights on to watch my potnas running trains on the girls. I was satisfied with having a pornographic view because I didn't have a desire to participate. I thought something was wrong with me because I was encouraging my friends to abuse someone's daughter. Shortly thereafter, that became my new normal.

When my sister found out what I was doing, she distanced herself from me and returned home to live with our mother. I tried to deny it, but my attempts to deceive her fell on deaf ears. I was ashamed of what I've done because I got caught not because it was wrong.

I decided to visit my mother to let her know that my sister would be returning home. When I arrived, she was entertaining a guest named Shannon, and to my dismay, my mother didn't ask me what happened, or what I'd done to make Tiffany want to come back home. I wanted to believe that her lack of concern was because she had company, but in my heart, I felt what I'd always felt; she didn't care, nor did she love me.

My mother's friend was beautiful, and I was very attracted to her. I decided to stay to see whether she used drugs. When she didn't, I set out to do everything in my power to sleep with her.

After my sister moved back home, Shannon began to visit my apartment frequently. She would immediately get undressed to show off her figure and her matching undergarments.

She took it slow with me, probably because I was her best friend's son. When we finally had sex, I thoroughly enjoyed it. I loved the way I felt inside of her and how she looked at me during intercourse.

I'd finally fallen in love—or what I thought was love. I started providing for her financially and I was crushed when I found out that she started sleeping with the insurance man.

Once again, a woman whom I used to love, I now hated. I cut off all communication with her—and my mother, as if my mom had played a part in her infidelity.

The second woman I fell in love with was Sandra, my cousin's friend. She was just as beautiful as Shannon but closer to my age. The only difference was I gave Sandra money. She demanded that I pay her to go behind the garage and grind on her butt. I didn't think that was right, but when you don't have anyone, anybody will do.

I was searching for something that was forever eluding me and that was love. The game Sandra played lasted only a short time. I grew bored with that because I was no longer a virgin and I wanted to have sex.

Getting girls or women at a young age was easy. Keeping girls or women at a young age were challenging. The girls my age soon realized that I didn't have any intention of being with them and that they would eventually have to sleep with my friends, and the women I was interested in weren't interested in me. I was tired of getting hurt, and if it hadn't been for my sister, I would have probably killed myself.

Currently Xavier was making garbage bags full of money and he was extremely powerful. One day he asked me a question and I yelled at him. It was unheard of for anyone to disrespect him—let alone his own employees, especially since we knew firsthand how dangerous he could potentially be.

He looked puzzled and said, "What's wrong?"

"I just want to die and I'm tired of this lifestyle."

"Meet me at Yancy's mortuary at 5:00 p.m.," he said. Then he left.

I was certain that he was going to kill me, but it didn't matter. I was already dead inside. I hated my mom, Shannon cheated on me, my sister abandoned me, and Sandra used me. So, it didn't matter what happened to me. I was empty.

I arrived an hour earlier than expected at the mortuary and I was waiting on Xavier. I brought my pistol because I thought it would be in my best interest to commit suicide rather than be brutally tortured and then murdered. When he finally arrived at the mortuary, he asked, "What's your problem?"

I responded with a question, "Why haven't you done anything about Brian's killer? You kept telling me not to worry about it, and you still haven't done anything. I even begged you and you constantly told me that you would handle it. Why haven't you handled it?"

He yelled, "I did!" and then he sat on the ground and tears welled up in his eyes. I was surprised because he was such a stoic character and always in control. He hugged me and then said, "Sometimes you need to remain silent, be aware of your surroundings, and listen, instead of always reacting like you do. You have eyes, but you clearly don't see."

Xavier hugged me again and asked, "Do you remember those two men?" My legs started shaking and I nodded yes. "They were Brian's killers. The first man in the bathroom was the trigger man, and I wanted you to see with your own eyes that this senseless murderer would not go unpunished." I thought by knowing this I would be set free, but instead, it amplified the guilt and the stronghold the devil had on me.

I never had experienced love and the love that Xavier was showing me had me so sick to my stomach until I threw up. I didn't believe that love could nauseate me, so in my heart I knew that definitely wasn't love.

I wanted to leave and told him that I didn't want to hear any more, and then he blurted out, "You lost one relative, but I lost both of my relatives. My first cousins at that." I could tell that he regretted killing his own flesh and blood, but he had made me a promise, and he kept it.

We cried and hugged one another. I tried to comfort the man whom I considered my father, and he tried to console his son. As we were leaving, he asked me if I wanted to ride across the Bay and go to San Francisco. "Sure," I said.

We pulled into this car lot and I thought that we were going to steal some cars because he asked me which one I liked. He opened the gate to the dealership and I pointed toward this convertible Corvette that was red with a white top.

The car was even equipped with speakers in the back of the seats. He gave me the car I'd chosen, but I didn't know how to drive. When he asked me, I simply replied, "Yes, I think so, but I've never driven before."

He gave me the keys, and after he locked up, we started drag racing across the Bay Bridge back to Oakland. When I reached my destination (home), I reflected on the events that had transpired and realized that Xavier did exactly what Rachel would do after she abused me. He tried to buy me, and at that moment, I had been bought with a vehicle.

My sister was about to graduate, and every beginning always has an end. My soul wasn't right with God, and what goes around usually comes back around.

# Chapter 12

## *Left for Dead*

The senseless murder of Xavier's relatives divided his family, and that sparked shoot-outs, and I was right in the middle of it. I tried to stay out the way by spending most of my time with this girl I'd met named Margie.

Margie dated a boy named Al who lived in another state, but when Al wasn't in town, we began to spend time together as friends. I didn't like Al because he had something that I wanted, so I became good friends with Margie. When they had problems, she would talk to me about them.

The more we talked the less apprehensive she was. A girl that attractive probably was use to guys trying to sleep with her, but I never gave her any inclination that was my main objective. I would always tell her to give him a chance and it would get better.

Communication was the key. She had gotten more comfortable around me and began to discuss intimate things about them. I would listen, but I didn't care one way or another about what she was going through. I only wanted to have sex with her to piss off Al.

Some women are destined for pain in their relationships because they ignore the warning signs. *What you want, and what they want can be contrary to one another.*

Margie started calling me more often when they would fight, asking me if she could come over. I always declined her offer, telling her, "You don't want to put yourself in a compromising predicament where you may regret doing something. You wouldn't want him to do that to you, so don't do it to him."

A couple of days would pass, and then they would be fighting again. This time I told her I would pick her up because she needed to get away. A scorned woman is an easy lay, yet a dangerous woman as well.

Immediately after she walked through the door, she was all over me. We had aggressive sex continuously, and she ended up spending the night. The next day I told everybody what happened and that shredded Margie to pieces.

Al finally got the news, and now he wanted to fight. This was what I'd planned, but all plans don't go as planned. It was supposed to have been a fair fight—if there ever is such a thing—but the fight was everything but fair.

It was night. I took my other cousins with me, Chris and Lee, and we followed his entourage to a place behind an elementary school that was next to a McDonald's. We left our guns in the car-- I was so ready to humiliate this dude. I started to approach him, and he lifted his shirt to signify that he wasn't carrying a gun and I did the same.

He tried to bull-rush me because I was quite a bit smaller than him, but I tripped him. I was pounding my fist into his face, but that didn't last long because someone grabbed me by the collar of my shirt and my pants and slammed me face down on the ground.

I thought that it might be the police—and then I realized I was being set up. People were coming out of abandoned cars and from behind bushes. Someone wrapped some sort of cloth around my neck. I couldn't hit anyone. The cloth was tightened, and I could breathe. I was gasping for air, understanding that I'd been set up, but I still didn't believe that my cousins were part of it. I need help, but my cousins stood by idled and watched.

"Why aren't they helping me? I must try to fight! I gotta fight!" I couldn't breathe, and they were dragging and hitting me! "Fight, I gotta fight! Kick, keep kicking," I thought to myself.

Now the fear of dying entered my mind, but I didn't want to die! "Scream!" I thought, but I couldn't scream for help because I couldn't breathe. I didn't want to die. Then they stabbed me. I knew I was hurt. I was hurt bad!

"I don't want to die! I'm not right with God! I don't wanna die!" I continued to say to myself.

I felt the knife piercing my skin. The white shirt I was wearing was soaked red by sweat and blood. I tried to protect my organs and that's when they slashed me across my face.

I put my left arm up to protect my face, and they slashed my wrist. I was fighting for my life. I continued to try to pull that cloth from around my neck while I was being choked, beaten, and sliced.

I was losing consciousness, and I thought, "If I pass out, they're going to kill me! Help me, Jesus! Help me! Help me, Jesus!" I literally could feel myself passing out. Either that, or I was close to dying because my eyes were closing involuntarily.

I got another glimpse of my cousins, and when I reached out to grab them by their pants legs, I thought, 'Surely, they're not going to let me die right before their eyes. I hope they at least show me some mercy because after all we're blood cousins.' And all the while, I kept thinking, *'Please, help me. Please?'*

As soon as I grabbed their pants, they stepped away from me. At that point, I didn't care any longer. I feared death, but nevertheless I gave up on living. The last thing I remembered was hearing a loud POW-- I was shot. I felt like I was dying. My skin was on fire as I lay there lifeless, drenched in blood!

It was all over for me, and my only thought was this: 'What is going to happen to my sister?' I had to take care of her. I thought about everything I had done wrong. I missed my cousin Brian. I thought about that little girl's hands I had squeezed, her brother whom I had severely beaten, the family's house I burned down, the pregnant lady and her daughter who had been kidnapped, her murdered husband, the torturing of Xavier's first cousins, the women I set out to be trained, as well as selling my own mother heroin.

But more than anything, I just wanted to be given another opportunity to tell my mama that I was sorry, and that after all the horror, I still loved her.

Lord, this couldn't be happening to me. I realized it was time to ask Jesus for forgiveness. I said, "Jesus, please forgive me for my sins. I'm sorry I did those things to those people." Then I lost consciousness.

The next thing I knew, a woman was telling me, "The ambulance is here. Just hang on." In a blur, I could make out her elderly face framed with gray-and-black hair. There was a crowd of people in the background, and I noticed a McDonald's sign. People were all around me and I didn't know if they were the same guys who had left me for dead or not.

I heard someone say, "He has lost a lot of blood and might require a blood transfusion! Oxygen, and let's get an IV started." I was too weak to say anything, but I sure thought, 'Oh no, no, no! No needles! Please, no needles. Just let me die. Please, God, do not let them do this to me! Please, God, no needles!'

I would rather have died than let them insert a needle into my arm. I could feel them tapping my right hand, but they couldn't get a good vein in my hand. Panic was overwhelming me, so I continued to pray. They finally started the IV, but the IV started backing up, and they had to redo it again. 'Not again, Lord Jesus, not again! Jesus, help me! Please, Jesus, no more needles! Jesus, help me please!'

Jesus did help me by sparing my life. All glory be to God for the mercy that He has shown me! *Take a moment and feel that!* A traumatized teen with a phobia of needles preferred death rather than accepting an IV—but God saved him.

The Bible states, "The sins of the mother and father are visited upon the children." And yet, I was saved!

I survived after calling on the name of the Lord, and my life was spared, but evil infiltrated my heart because I was ready to kill. I was blessed to have only a flesh wound, but it pained me to be beaten and left for dead behind a dumpster in a McDonald's parking lot.

How cruel can someone be? Often after we get what we want from the Lord, we immediately turn our backs on God. My attitude changed once I knew that I was going to live. I was not going to let this go! They had to pay! How dare they!

I was taught the wrong way to live. I was taught how to kill, but now I thought I had to kill just to remain alive. I was heartbroken because of what my cousins had done, and either I was going to kill them, or I knew that they were going to try to kill me.

When I was finally released from the hospital, Xavier threw me a homecoming. I wasn't interested in a party. I wanted to stay home and spend time with my sister. I told my sister to continue to do right even though I knew I was going to do wrong.

She assumed I was going to take vengeance into my own hands and even though she promised to visit me, she knew it would be better for her to stay away and live with our mom. That was best, but nevertheless, it didn't stop me from being disappointed and distraught.

*Déjà vu once again.* Again, I coped by placing the sheets in my mouth, screaming from the depths of my soul, rocking back in forth in a fetal position. Although, it was different people, and different problems, the ending result was the same—death!

I was tired of this lifestyle. My only reason for indulging in this type of activity had been to rescue my sister, but since she was no longer in harm's way, why did I continue to perpetuate such a dysfunctional and violent existence?

After all I'd seen, I couldn't believe that I'd done so much wrong that I was beyond redemption. But *Evil Eyes* (the devil) would like us to believe that we're too far-gone.

The Word of God says, "For I am persuaded that neither death nor life, nor angels nor principalities nor powers, nor things present nor things to come, nor height nor depth, nor any other created thing, shall be able to separate us from the love of God, which is in Christ Jesus our Lord" (Rom. 8:38–39).

Does Jesus really save sinners? I wanted to give my life to God, but every time that I did, I took it back out of his hands. This time, it was my desire to kill my cousins that drove me from God. I was sure that if I didn't do anything to them, they would do something to me.

My flesh said, "Kill them," but my spirit said, "Forgive them." Where was my faith? I had none. Hebrews 11:1 says, "Now faith is the substance of this hope for the evidence of things not seen."

I didn't have faith because I didn't trust Him. How can you trust a stranger? *If you don't have a relationship with God, how can you trust Him. We were taught at a young age not to trust strangers. If we don't know God, is it possible to have faith. "So then faith comes by hearing, and hearing by the Word of God" Romans 10:17.*

I'd always been dealt the short end of the stick, and I had to know exactly how things were going to turn out; because I had grown accustomed to being forced to endure the unexpected if I didn't take control. *But are we really in control? I think not!*

I'd seen too much death, and although I didn't want to kill them, my body and face were slightly disfigured. I was stitched and scarred in various places, therefore, I was determined to repay an evil for an evil. What other choice did I have? (Forgive)

*Everyone has scars from what they have encountered in life, but one day those scars will no longer cause us pain. Although the scar is present, the pain is absent.*

*I'm called to forgive, and I know Jesus forgives all sinners who come to repentance (murderers, rapists, child molesters, drug dealers, prostitutes, everyone).*

Our past, present, and future sins have already been washed clean by the blood of Jesus. Even knowing all of this, I still did the unimaginable. It's disheartening to have nothing to say now except, "May my relatives rest in peace." *Lord have mercy on my soul!*

# Chapter 13

## *Need to Get Out*

The next day after getting home, considering the role I played in the death of my cousins, I realized I needed to get away from my family members, so I headed to Marvin's house.

Marvin was one of my best friends who lived a couple of houses down from my great-grandmother Janice. Marvin asked me how I was doing and if I had heard about what had happened to Al. I could tell that he was concerned, but I didn't want to relive that tragedy again, so I allowed my silence to speak for me.

I was emotionless, because I lacked the ability to feel anything except evil and coldness which resided in my heart. By this time, I'd done, seen, and participated in too much death and destruction of God's people. Sympathy was no longer a word in my vocabulary. I didn't want to feel this type of pain any longer, so I did what my mom, dad, and many others trapped within the periphery of poverty and hatred do to escape grief. I medicated myself with marijuana and alcohol.

I called Xavier to let him know my whereabouts, and he advised me to stay at Marvin's until he picked me up. For some reason, he kept repeating, "Make sure you stay at Marvin's."

He knew that I was quick tempered and lacked self-control because often I would be led by my emotions. He probably thought that my emotions were going to overtake me, but I reassured him that I wasn't going to do anything, even though he knew I would take great pleasure in harming if not killing Al.

I began to feel uncomfortable at Marvin's house, so I called Xavier to let him know that I was leaving. Then, the little peace I did have dissipated, and guilt consumed me.

I was responsible for the extinction of my cousins. I didn't want to believe that my relatives, with whom I had grown up with were dead and that the guys who had inflicted pain and almost killed me were still alive.

I tried to console myself by justifying my actions, saying, "They tried to have me killed." But that was a lie because even *when we choose the lesser of two evils, we're still choosing evil.* At times, it's easier for us to believe a lie rather than deal with the truth because the truth exposes who we truly are rather than who we pretend to be.

The Holy Bible states in James 1:23–24, "For if anyone is a hearer of the word and not a doer, he is like a man observing his natural face in a mirror; for he observes himself, goes away, and immediately forgets what kind of man he was."

I was trying to sell myself a lie that I couldn't buy. This is what the devil tries to do to us daily. He would rather deceive us and have us disillusioned, believing in the creature rather than the Creator of all things—God.

I had a Christian background, but I chose to live in darkness rather than the light, because men love the darkness when they fear their deeds will be exposed by the light. (Truth)

The Bible states, "For the wages of sin is death" (Romans 6:23) and if you really think about it, wages are something that you earn. I was earning death: total separation from the Lord and an unending baptism by hellfire, but the gift of God is eternal life.

We're either going to live our life for God or for the devil. *You must choose one.* In my world thus far, I could envision no in-between. We are supposed to love God with all our heart, mind, and soul, not primarily by what we say but by how we live. *Many of us travel down a stairway headed straight toward that dreadful doorway labeled WELCOME TO HELL, where the DEAD RESIDES!*

Instead of leaving Marvin's house, I decided to stay there, and Xavier picked me up shortly thereafter our last conversation. He told me what happened to Al and that he would never look the same. He had evidently taken great pleasure in harming that child.

Al was my age, and I felt more guilt now than ever before. This was a never-ending cycle, one that trapped me until I saw Al, and I didn't feel guilty any longer!

I can recall seeing Al at school, and I would smile because he couldn't look me directly in the face. Al had been severely beaten with a pistol until it crushed the bones in his face.

---

Margie told me that he had to have surgery to get a permanent plate inserted in his face. I felt remorse because for the rest of his life, he would be permanently disfigured. *Was it worth it? I think not!* That changed me because from that day on, I didn't take pleasure in anyone's pain or misfortune.

I wanted to apologize to Al, but I didn't think that he wanted to hear from me. Nor did I know how I would go about doing it. Xavier wasn't pleased with the change he saw in me, but he realized that this life wasn't for me. My life took a drastic change from being abused, to an abuser, and even a murderer. I hated what I once loved, and I wanted out!

Xavier tried to give me a way out by introducing me to some Chinese businessmen who needed investors for a pharmaceutical company they were in the process of opening.

I met with these guys at Rachel's home, and they wanted some silent partners to initially invest large sums of money in their startup company. Then invest monthly to assist with the company's overhead. I wasn't equipped at that age to make an intelligent and informed decision, so I declined their offer.

That was my escape and I didn't recognize it. According to 1 Corinthians 10:13, "No temptation has overtaken you except such as common to man; but God is faithful, who will not allow you to be tempted beyond what you are able, but with the temptation will also make the way of escape, that you may be able to bear it."

I preferred to spend thousands on materialistic items that I didn't need, nor would I gain any profit from them. Or I'd keep my money idle in my pockets or safes instead of investing in a legitimate business that would have brought me additional revenue.

Since I had been taught well and was good at selling drugs, I called Xavier and asked for his blessing to branch off from his empire. I naively thought there would be no better way to escape than to work for myself—or better yet, have someone work for me.

I knew some high school students who wanted me to give them jobs. So once Zay gave me the okay, I put together my own team and rented a small apartment for Marcus, Isaiah, and Andrew on the outskirts of the city. There weren't any shoot-outs and most importantly, there weren't any more killings!

I liked Andrew better than the others because he played basketball well and we would go to different parks to play basketball. I gave him wisdom like Xavier gave me wisdom, but my judgment wasn't as good as Zay's because although I had experience, it wasn't enough.

Rachel would tell me that Andrew was jealous of me and that she didn't trust him. She said, "Marcus and especially Isaiah will be faithful to you like you were to Xavier. But please be careful of Andrew."

I thought I knew it all and I used her addiction against her by saying, "What can an addict tell me?" I ignored one of the rules that I had been taught and that was to not turn a deaf ear to any information until it was confirmed or denied.

One day at the basketball court in Walnut Creek, I met this guy who was selling some counterfeit twenty-dollar bills. They looked real, but they all had the same serial number on them. He introduced me to a scheme that involved washing them at fast-food restaurants and nightclubs.

He cautioned me never to go to the bar but always go to the waitresses. The waitresses who drinks alcohol and takes shots preferably are the best.

I asked how much he had, and he said $200,000, but he was letting them go for $50,000. I told him that I needed to talk to Xavier first and I would get back with him.

Xavier had some contacts in Seattle, and he knew girls that worked for a Canadian money exchange, and they could possibly assist me with my endeavor. I gave the guy from Walnut Creek what he charged me, and I started making plans to travel to Seattle.

First, I bought a sports utility vehicle and I carefully placed the money inside the door panels of the vehicle. Monica was my girlfriend at the time and she was willing to go with me.

I had met Monica at a Taco Bell restaurant in Benicia. She was about five feet two, half Asian and half Caucasian. She had reddish-brown hair, a large bust, and a round firm butt. She was beautiful. She had on some fitted white dress slacks. I still love white pants today because of her. I thought that she was a business lady at first until I did a background check on her.

I found out that we had the same profession. She was a drug dealer, but she sold drugs in San Mateo. I asked Xavier about her, and he said, "She's a keeper!" I didn't know exactly what he meant by that, but I wasn't going to let her go regardless.

She sold drugs because she was responsible for providing for her siblings because her parents abandoned them. I instantly fell in love with that woman. We both wanted something better for our families, regardless of what we had to do.

Xavier told me to be careful because she wasn't afraid to use a gun. There had been an incident in which she shot and killed and intruder. Someone tried to kick her door in and instead of robbing her he got himself killed.

After the police carefully searched her home, they found $12,000 cash and a couple of pounds of marijuana. The intruder died from his gunshot wounds, but the police ruled the shooting a justifiable homicide. Unfortunately, he was known for robbing and breaking into people's homes.

I finally had someone whom I could relate to, but I still felt sympathy for the young man who lost his life. I was perplexed about the incident, because I didn't want my girlfriend harmed. *You never know the situation he was placed in that pushed him into doing what he was doing. When we feel like we don't have any choices then we don't..*

Some people choose robbery, while others might choose selling drugs, or prostitution. We deceive ourselves to believe that this was our only option. Like I previously stated, "'When we choose the lesser of two evils, we're still choosing evil.'" Satan blinds our minds to the effects and nature of sin and the consequences at that moment. We can prepare to sin, but we're not in control of the consequences.

Regardless of what negative choice we might make, it will never get us where we want to be. According to the Bible in Proverbs 1:19 says, "So are the ways of everyone who is greedy for gain; it takes away the life of its owners." Far too many people prefer microwave solutions rather than trusting and waiting on God's blessings.

Monica was different than those other girls I've dated. We got along very well—after all, we had the same interests. She was compassionated and had a nurturing side that I was attracted to.

I didn't like selling drugs, although I was reluctant to stop. I wanted Monica to stop, but she was also unwilling to do so. Therefore, I decided to visit the places where she was selling drugs to ensure her safety.

Her attire was different when she was selling, and she looked completely different from the woman I had met at Taco Bell. She wore baggy clothes, and you could barely distinguish her from a male.

She had a razor in her mouth and carried a pistol. She was far from that beautiful woman dressed in white slacks, but I found her transformation impressive. She was playing the part.

Wherever I was at, Monica was there also. She had grown quite fond of my mom and would visit her without me. For some odd reason, she loved my mother. I never knew why she wanted to visit her often, but we were there daily.

I started using Rachel's house to catch up on sleep. I always slept on the couch in the living room instead of my bedroom because of the bad memories stemming from my childhood.

I couldn't sleep peacefully because of the noise that Monica and Rachel made. I figured they were drunk because they consumed a lot of beer and played cards.

A part of me was jealous because for years, I had longed for my mother to show me love, but I wasn't selfish enough to spoil their fun. So, I sat back and listened to the jokes they told each other.

I never knew that my mother had that type of personality and I enjoyed seeing her softer side. Then one day, jealously entered my heart, and I said, "Monica, you have to be careful around your new best friend because she just might hold you down by your hands and let drug dealers and addicts have rape you."

By shouting that, I thought I would break their bond, but it did the opposite. Monica was upset with me, and instead of having sympathy for what Tiffany and I had endured, she embraced Rachel and said, "God has forgiven you for your past."

I was so pissed. I stormed out of the house, and Monica ran after me. I told her to go back inside because she didn't have a clue what Rachel had done to us! She replied, "You told me what she did, and everybody has a past. No one is perfect but God and therefore we all have made our fair share of mistakes. You have to forgive her to be forgiven."

Matthew 6:14–15 says, "For if you forgive men their trespasses, your heavenly Father will also forgive you. But if you don't forgive men their trespasses, neither will your Father forgive your trespasses."

She asked me to look at my mother's life through her eyes: The beatings she received at the hands of my father, the women at the funeral, not being the beneficiary of the insurance policy, and having stepchildren she had had no knowledge of.

Then Monica had the audacity to bring up the mistakes that I'd made, like killing my own flesh and blood, the family I'd tried to burn alive. She hurt me the most when she said that I was responsible for Brian's death.

I said, "F—— you," and I started walking off, but once again she chased me.

Then, she asked why I never asked her why she cried when I first told her about what happened to my sister and me. I didn't have anything to say, so I simply asked her to leave me alone. She repeated the question.

"Okay, Monica. I assumed you were hurting because I was hurting."

"No, that's not the reason! I was Tiffany!" she exclaimed.

"What?"

"I was Tiffany, but my mother didn't wait until I was twelve years old! I was six! I was six years old! Do you hear me? That's why I asked you if you wanted kids! Because I can't have any! The one thing I was created for, I can't do! I can't give you any children!" she exclaimed.

I felt rage, but most of all I felt her pain! I was shaking my head from side to side in disbelief. I hugged and kissed her, and we cried. Monica loved being by the water, so we drove to the lake in silence. But when we finally arrived at our destination, she started to cry again uncontrollably.

Just when I thought that the worst was over, she said, "I blame myself for my mom's absence. I tried to convince her that it wasn't her fault. When I forgave my mom, I realized that it was the drugs. I knew that she still loved her children, but that's when she left."

"I'm sorry to hear that."

"Two years later, she called and told us that she loved us and that she always would." Then she was silent.

"What? Monica, what? Are you okay? What, babe?"

"She committed suicide!"

"What?"

"She killed herself, and it's my fault! It's all my fault! I blame myself! I killed my mom!"

I couldn't conjure up any words to say. I was speechless, and all the life that I had left, and that wasn't that much. I was looking at her, and I wanted to hold her, but images of my mother dying infiltrated my mind.

I remember staring at Monica, but I was looking through her seeing my mother dying by her own hands. I was tired of this type of lifestyle because I was once close to death, but now I was revisiting death through someone else eyes.

Once the silence was broken, she said, "I cater to your mother because of the guilt I feel about my own mother and that's why I cling to her. I just want her to have a little happiness before she passes away. Am I wrong for that? Am I wrong for wanting someone to have a little peace in this world before they die? Some people die in misery. I don't want that for your mother."

I didn't respond because I felt horrible. Here was my woman who would have done anything to get her mother back, and I had purposely kept my mother sick and plotted to kill her.

I was finally exposed, and I didn't like what I saw in myself. I was generating negative energy and empowering it by selling my own mama drugs. When the reality set in of what I was doing I hated myself. I missed my mother and I had a strong desire to hug her and tell her that I loved her.

We rushed to my mama's house and we all cried. I told her that I apologized for selling her drugs and for trying to kill her. It startled her, but it didn't surprise her. I said, "Please forgive me! Will you forgive me?"

Mama, Monica, and I hugged each other and cried periodically until the following morning. From that day forward, I'm proud to say my mama never touched another needle again!

At last, she put her children over her addiction. She's clean and still praising God. It took years for me to forgive myself for keeping my own mother sick.

I told Mama we were still leaving for Seattle soon, but when we got settled, I was going to send for her. Then Monica told me to ask her instead of telling her, and when I did, my mother said, "Yes." She told us to be careful and that she would pray for us!

I said, "I love you, Mama."

And she answered, "I love you too, son."

For the first time in my life she validated my existence. I finally had peace in my heart because I knew for once that I mattered, and she loved me too. Finally, Mama had said those magic words I'd spent my life waiting to hear, *"I love you too, son."*

# Chapter 14

## *Bad Things Must End*

The day finally arrived when Monica and I were heading to Seattle. We decided to give the counterfeit money a test run by spending the money in various cities on our way to Seattle. We were spending money at gas stations, clubs, bars, and restaurants. I was surprised how easy it was to spend the money without encountering any problems whatsoever.

It took us three days to get there and our intention was to remain focused on the job at hand. We immediately called the Canadian girls, Mary and Chloe.

Mary gave us a tour, and she showed us a couple of places that we could stay, but I wasn't comfortable with those places. I refused to stay directly in the city where I was going to flood that city with drugs and counterfeit currency.

Mary was more laid back than Chloe, but Chloe was money hungry. We hadn't even settled in yet, and she wanted to drive to Canada and start washing the money. I let her know that she wasn't running this operation and a rush decision could have horrific consequences.

After all, I wanted to rest from our drive. I wanted my mind to be rested prior to engaging in any criminal activity. Plus, I refused to place my fate in the hands of a stranger. Only a fool would place his freedom in the hands of a stranger, and neither Monica nor I was a fool.

We found a city that we were comfortable with and it was close to Canada. We decided to stay in Bellingham. This was a quiet town and it appeared that the citizens there minded their own business. We leased a town house and Monica loved it. Before we could fully decorate it, we decided to head to Canada.

On our way there, Chloe told us that we had to exchange our American money for Canadian money and that's when I knew exactly how we were going to get rid of the money. Mary was somewhat nervous, and I believed that she would fold under pressure if something went wrong.

She also had friends who worked at the Canadian money exchange. I wasn't going to let her exchange money for that reason. Her friends were people who didn't know anything about me, and I liked that idea better. I held a brief conversation with her friends at a club called Oasis.

These women were basically party women who loved to drink and have sex with African American men. They smoked a little weed and they would occasionally do a line of cocaine, but other than that they were average women.

I convinced them to help us exchange the money and I figured we probably would have a two-day run, for sure, and we would be pushing it on the third day, depending on when they made their deposits.

The challenge we had was getting the money into Canada because they had x-ray machines at the border that could see inside the vehicle's door panel. And at times they would randomly search the vehicles by opening the hood and the trunk.

But I believed that the reward was worth the risk. The greater the risk usually means the greater the reward, and that was a chance that I was willing to take.

I wasn't going to put Monica's or the other women freedom in jeopardy because I knew if I got caught that I wouldn't tell on myself. Therefore, I felt that it would behoove me to drive through the checkpoint alone.

I installed a bicycle rack on top of the vehicle and purchased two bicycles to place there. I bought a baby seat and an ice chest, which I placed in the back seat. If I was stopped, my plan was to tell them my girlfriend and I were vacationing, and we were the proud parents of a healthy baby boy!

I arrived at the border, and I had Monica, Chloe, and Mary follow me in two separate vehicles. I admit I was nervous, and I believed that I looked guilty. The border patrol asked me a couple of questions, briefly glanced inside the vehicle, and then said, "Be safe, and enjoy your stay."

I took a deep breath as I proceeded through the checkpoint and said, "I made it!" I was prideful, and I praised myself by saying, "I'm the man!" (foolish vanity.) Many of us boast when we get away with crime or sin, but sin is something that we should strive to get rid of, not something that we should strive to get away with.

We stayed at a hotel for a couple of days because I didn't feel comfortable with exchanging money that soon. I wanted to reprogram the girls' minds to the way I wanted them to think. I'd never been one who wanted to rule by fear instead, I wanted to rule by fact—I was going to completely inform them of what their job description was and tell them about the risks.

By doing so, that cleared my conscience just in case our plans didn't go as expected. They knew prior to doing anything exactly what they were getting involved in. They knew the pros and the cons as well as the ins and the outs. For every risk, there's always a consequence.

After I thoroughly instructed them, I said, "It's your choice, but choose wisely. No one knows your situation better than you, and if you have children you can't tolerate being away from, then this just might not be the best job opportunity for you."

I gave them another choice because if they didn't feel comfortable with doing the job, they could recruit someone to do it for them. It didn't take them long to recruit people, but I wasn't dealing with the people they recruited.

I had Mary and Chloe pay their own people while Monica ensured that they did. The girls paid them because I felt my job was completed when I drove the money across the border and I refused to put any money into anyone's hands.

Everything was in order, and the girls were knowledgeable about the deceptive roles they would play, so we were ready to conduct business. We exchanged almost $180,000 in less than two days.

Monica and I left Canada late that same evening. I decided we would only change a certain amount of Canadian money back to American currency. I didn't feel comfortable with trying to exchange a large amount of money at one time, plus I could also exchange some of the currency back to American currency in Seattle.

The relationship between my mother and I had been repaired, so I wired her some money through Western Union. We visited that store quite often, and Monica befriended the employee who wired the money for us.

Since I was the one who filled out the forms, I noticed at the bottom of the form that the individual who was receiving the money didn't have to show identification if they knew the answer to the test question. Here I go again—hatching another plot for riches.

Because Monica befriended the girl, I had Monica talk to her about her financial status to see if she was in financial crisis. Many people compromise their beliefs and values when their resources run dry. The employee was on board, so we started wiring money to ourselves in various cities before driving to a Western Union location in another city to pick it up the money.

We had different people send the maximum while someone else picked up the money, and I paid them 25 percent of the gross. We hit probably every store location that was equipped with a Western Union.

I started missing my mother, and I asked her if she would come visit us, but my intention was for her to permanently move with us. She enjoyed Seattle, but she rarely left the house. She had developed a strong and personal relationship with God and God took alcohol out of her heart. Now my mother was alcohol and drug free. Glory to God!

I leased mom a town house right across the street from mine. My mama loved Monica and wanted me to marry her, but I was in fear of marriage. I thought that was too much responsibility for me at such a young age. Plus, honestly, I didn't think that I would live that long.

Monica and I would go out and party every day after working hours. We were in love and having a good time. This was the happiest time of my life. I had my mother and my woman by my side. I missed my sister, but my relationship with her had become strained after all the violence.

Fortunately, all bad things must end and thank God that they do. God allows us to be wounded in order for us to seek healing from Him. We can only do wrong for so long, and whom He loves, He chastens.

Monica and I decided to go to this club in Kirkland called the Dragon Palace. We spent a little less than $1000 there. We had almost got rid of all the counterfeit money, and we were blessed not to get caught in the process.

I decided to give Mary and Chloe the remaining money and instructed them not to go to the Dragon Palace because we had just gone there a couple of days ago. After the fact, I let them know that it would probably be beneficial if they stopped altogether.

My conscience was clear because I had warned them, but I was determined to get all that money out of my possession.

As soon as the girls left, I had bad feeling about going out therefore, we stayed home and played board games with mama. Those girls I warned not to go to the same club completely disregarded my warning. By this time, the feds had various agents in that club looking for the culprits who had flooded the Pacific Northwest and Canada with counterfeit money.

The police already caught the guy, from whom I purchased the money, and he was incarcerated awaiting trial, and naturally like most do, he decided to cooperate with the police. He didn't know my name, nor did he have any idea where I was residing.

The only way that they could trace the money was because the counterfeit bills had identical serial numbers on each bill. I called Zay, and he instructed me to burn the remaining money and flush the ashes.

I remembered that I had some money at Mama's house, and instead of burning the money like I asked her to, she tore it into small pieces and flushed them down the toilet. The currency turned the toilet bowl red. I hadn't been arrested yet, so it was quite possible that the girls hadn't rolled on me.

I continued going about my daily activities as normal.
I was introduced to a guy named Will who had some great prices on cocaine. I thought I would purchase a large amount from him, but something didn't seem right, so I declined his offer, which was a *too-good-to-be-true deal.*

As soon as I left the apartment building and tried to get into my vehicle, I was hit with flashing lights. I was unable to drive, so I exited the vehicle and went into a dead sprint. I was running down an alleyway when I ran straight into a police officer.

He seemed afraid of me, just as I was afraid of him. He got a great look at my face, but somehow, I was able to elude him and get away. I jumped a ten-foot brick wall and ran across the freeway.

There were police everywhere! My adrenaline was rushing so much that I ran through a wooden fence. I immediately got up off the ground, still running, and hid in a boathouse. I crawled as far as I could up under this boat. I was scared, my heart was racing, and I didn't have a clue exactly where I was. I could hear the policemen talking and shining their flashlights all around the boathouse. But for reasons unknown, they never searched the boathouse.

After hours of nervousness and fear, I called a close friend of mine to whom I sold drugs to and asked him to pick me up. I should have called Monica, but I didn't want to involve her because I wanted to keep her protected.

I told Cedric what happened and asked him if I could use him as my alibi. He agreed, and I thought he was solid. My alibi would be that I was at Cedric's house. It was a good alibi I thought, at the time.

He picked me up in his Subaru Legacy and I hopped in his trunk. He let the back seats down to ensure that I was receiving enough air to breathe. I explained to him again what happened, and he said that he was okay with that.

From that moment on, I wasn't afraid of anything. It would be just like what Xavier said: you make the bed that you lie in, and when you get up, you must be certain that it's put perfectly back into place. So, I was confident that I was doing the right thing.

The following day, Mama called and said, "A Mr. Tim Robertson from the Secret Service is here at my house and he's looking for you. He wants to know if you will meet him here and son, I think that you should come home."

I was riding with one of the neighbors and as we drove by mama's house and we noticed white men in trench coats standing by three black sport utility vehicles. My driver said, "That's the feds;" I agreed and told him that I wasn't in a hurry to go home and deal with that mess. *If you don't address your problems, your problems will address you.*

We drove a few more blocks before we were pulled over and I was arrested. They took me to the police station and tried to intimidate me—they did a good job. They told me that I was looking at 245 years in a federal prison, but I was more focused on how they knew about the apartment where I used to live in Antioch, California.

I was confused, and I believed that multiple people must have talked. I was almost certain that Mary and Chloe snitched, and rest assured, they did exactly what I thought they would do. Especially after the feds told them that they wouldn't be able to visit the United States any longer.

I wasn't admitting to anything because I knew that my bed was properly made because they didn't find any money in my possession or dwellings.

Tim Robertson had me writing page after page after page of different sentences and different letters of the alphabet, various names, and different cities. I was very familiar with the names because most of those names and locations were where we either sent or received money through Western Union transfers. I wasn't ignorant to their devices.

They were conducting a handwriting sample for analysis, but I didn't fill out any forms. So, there was no possible way that my handwriting could be linked to any of the Western Union forms.

After that, the officer informed me that one of the students whom I had selling drugs for me had snitched on me. Come to find out he went to a girl's apartment to have sex with her and when she wasn't home they decided to steal furniture from her apartment. I sent him on an assignment and he had the audacity to venture off from the task at hand to have sex. *(Common sense isn't that common for some people).*

He had over $3,000 in his pockets and he was stealing end tables, lamps, and chairs. For the life of me, I couldn't understand that at all. He was a thief and just like an addict, he couldn't stop getting high from stealing.

Just because you're not actively practicing a bad habit doesn't mean that the habit has dissipated. *Do we really know what resides in us? What was he thinking?* I told him to go pick up a package and take it back to the house and someone would come and pick it up later. That was it! That was all he had to do!

Some people will purposely go to the store and have the money to buy what they desire, but they will still choose to steal. I wanted to strangle him! Because majority of these unnecessary problems could have been avoided by following instructions. Or so I thought?

He was caught because he was loading the vehicle with white socks on his hands. A neighbor saw that they had socks covering their hands and she called the police. Once he was caught, he told them everything. Luckily, they didn't have enough evidence to charge me because there weren't any drugs in the apartment or in my vehicle.

They extradited me back to California because the guy I bought the money from needed to identify me. Instead of incarcerating me in Alameda County, they took me to Commons County jail.

I was fighting daily because I believed in my heart that the devil wanted me dead. I called Zay because I was frantic and told him what was going on. I was held without bail because they wanted me to roll on Xavier. I told him I was solid, and he hired Chris Sicman to represent me.

One thing about Chris—he was willing to be paid in drugs. He enjoyed snorting pencil-size lines of cocaine. During our first meeting, I was primarily concerned with getting a bail and his chief concern was how he wanted to be paid-cocaine.

I didn't know how long I would last in Commons County Jail. The fighting along with the stress were taking a toll on me. Xavier told me to be strong, and as soon as I was given a bond, he was going to bond me out.

Reality sets in fast when you're incarcerated. The things that you take for granted are the very things that you miss and cherish. All the things that you have said, done, and contemplated doing finally comes to an end when you're incarcerated.

I advised Chris to give my sister and mama complete control over my money and to give my sister all my jewelry. I also asked mama to make sure Monica was safe. I made a conscience decision that I am willing to lie in the same bed that I messed up.

After four months or so, my days began to get better. Xavier knew a guy named Dillon who was currently at the same jail as me. He was a *Trustee*, one who could somewhat move around the facility. He was 5ft 8inches tall but around two hundred and eighty pounds. Somehow, I was blessed to be moved into a cell with his cousin named Will. I had some backup, so I didn't mind walking the yard doing recreational time.

One day on the yard, they were telling me about the Smith brothers from Kirkland. One of the brothers ran into a work out facility and killed about eight people that stole from him, but four others got away. He ran outside in broad daylight and killed the remaining four in their vehicle. They told me that they couldn't wait to introduce me to him because they used to be business partners before they got locked up.

I began to wonder how people viewed me. I might have seen and indulged in my fair share of criminal activity, but surely, I didn't think that I was like them, but clearly from what they heard, I was exactly like them.

I battled their observation in my mind and heart, and I kept saying that my grandfather was a pastor, and I loved God! They can't believe that

I'm like them, or then again, maybe I am. According to John 1:6, "If we say that we have fellowship with Him, and walk in darkness, we lie and do not the Truth." *Shouldn't we love God by how we live and not primarily by what we say? What fellowship does darkness and light have together? None.*

I went back to my cell early that night, and here I go again (my readers should know the drill), placing the sheets in my mouth, screaming at the top of my lungs, but crying dry tears! Yet again, in a different place, but the same results!

I met with my lawyer and told him that I desperately needed to get out of jail, but he stated that he had some good news and bad news. My first inclination was, "They were going to pin some murders on me" but he told me that I was given bail. I could handle any news after that because I believed now my peace would return. "Okay, tell Xavier to bail me out."

"You have a one million cash bond and Zay wanted the bail to be around $500,000." I was shocked because I've always been honest with Zay, and I've never stolen anything from him. He told me he would bail me out now his story is changing!

I couldn't believe that he wasn't keeping his word. He'd always kept his word. I didn't want to sound too upset though because I knew my lawyer would relay my displeasure back to Xavier, then he would probably have me killed.

I wasn't giving up, but I was mentally preparing myself for the long haul of being incarcerated. I was finally in the system and I couldn't do a whole lot being locked up. I needed help from someone in order for me to have hope.

The help that I needed didn't reside in Xavier, Monica, Tiffany, or even my Mother. The help that I desperately needed could only be found in Jesus Christ. When all else fails (the world which will fail you), then it was time for me to call on Jesus Christ. He was the only one who could make a way out of no way.

The Bible states, "The things which are impossible with men are possible with God" (Mark 18:27). Sometimes we must be placed in isolation to receive revelation. Even when we give up, God never gives up on us!

# Chapter 15

## *God Delivered Me*

I knew Jesus Christ wouldn't fail me. HE would hear my cry. I wished that my life was different, but it was what I had made it. I seriously thought that it was over for me. *Our choices yesterday lead us to where we are today.* I started to give up on my freedom.

I requested a Bible, and I started reading it throughout the day. I prayed and mediated on the Word of God. It was like His words were jumping off the page and right into my heart.

My family was a praying family, and prayer changes things. After all, I knew in my head that I was not like them, but my heart was dark, and only God knew how black that darkness was.

I developed a relationship with God and drew close to God when I was incarcerated, but as soon as I was able to make bail, like so many others, I ran away from Him. *We call on Him for help in our time of trouble, and when He sees us through, do you turn our back on Him?* I know I did. I praised His name in jail, and when He opened the cell gates, I was worse than before.

*The Bible states in Luke 11:24–26, "When an unclean spirit goes out of a man, he goes through dry places, seeking rest; and finding none, he says, 'I will return to my house from which I came.' And when he comes, he finds it swept and put in order.*

*Then he goes and takes with him seven other spirits more wicked than himself, and they enter and dwell there; and the last state of that man is worse than the first."*

That's known as jailhouse religion. I figured it was a strong possibility that I was going to prison, so I had to make money so that I could afford to have the witnesses exterminated.

As fast as I made money, I spent money. I wasn't out of jail long before I had to go back to Seattle. Since it was a federal case, my attorney was taking that case as well. We would go to his hotel room to discuss the case, and he would be high on cocaine. *The risk that some people are willing to take with your life might not line up with your willingness to be placed at risk.*

Did he realize that while he was getting high my life was on the line? I wasn't pleased with what he was indulging in at all. I started wondering whether it was a good idea for him to be representing me.

Here I go again in need of Jesus hoping that His grace would abound and not His wrath. I was using God's grace like it was free, but it wasn't free because it cost Jesus Christ His life.

My family depended on me for support and I had to beat this case. My first thought about being convicted was, "What would happen to my mama?" I wondered whether she would return to heroin to escape from the pain of having her only son in prison.

My trial was in a couple of weeks and my attorney still hadn't got in contact with my alibi, Cedric. Chris was leaving numerous messages, but Cedric wasn't returning any of his phone calls. And when he did, he made some excuse about being too busy to discuss the case.

Zay was concerned, and I tried to assure him that Cedric was solid, even if I knew in my heart that he wasn't. I told him that I explained the situation to Eric before he picked me up, so he knew what transpired. Xavier stated, "So did the girls and look how that turned out! If you don't handle it, I will!"

A couple of days passed, and we lost all communication with Cedric because he turned his phone off. "I will kill him if he doesn't come through!" I thought.

Later that evening, my attorney received a phone call from him saying, "I can't perjure myself! If they find out that I'm lying, my life will be over too." There goes my alibi.

He apologized to me and told me that he just couldn't risk it all over a lie. We were all in shock! Chris immediately called Xavier and before he could say anything, I said "No! Never again would I kill, nor did I want it done for me. So please no!"

It was a struggle within me not to harm Eric, but enough was enough. I was beginning to see the light. At this time, all I wanted to do was spend my last days with my mama and my sister. I began to distance myself from Xavier and even Monica. I didn't want her implicated in anything, so I made her part ways with me until my trial was over.

She had the nerve to tell my mama that she would take the charges for me, but I refused to let that happen. Then again, what some people say and what they will do may differ. She could have been just talking.

My lawyer advised me of the predicament we were facing for trial and thoroughly explained that he had to change his strategy in a matter of days. Then he insinuated that he was going to need some help staying up.

I knew what he wanted, and I didn't want to give him any more cocaine, but nevertheless, I reluctantly did. He extended the trial date to give us a few more weeks, and then news of what happened to Cedric came in. Cedric had been in a motorcycle accident, and he was in critical condition fighting for his life.

I immediately called Xavier and asked him if he had anything to do with it, but he replied, "No!" He told me that I was my own man and that he honored and respected my request—even if he knew that it was a bad decision. I believed him, and I never questioned him about Cedric again.

Thank God, Cedric survived, and he was rehabilitating in San Diego, California. I didn't want any more blood or death on my conscience. My trial was convening in a couple of days, and we were going over my questions repeatedly.

By this time, I had probably lost fifty pounds due to stress. The day of the trial came, and the prosecution called their first witness, who was the police officer who had clearly seen my face when we startled each other.

The State's Attorney asked him if he could identify the person seen running from the vehicle, and he said, "Yes." He told the jury that he had gotten a good look at my face, and beyond a shadow of a doubt I was the one fleeing from the vehicle.

He went on to say that we alarmed one another at one point during the chase. He stated that he had been a police officer for seventeen years, and he was absolutely positive that it was me fleeing the scene.

My heart sank because he was believable. It wasn't necessary for him to be believable because he wasn't lying. The truth never changes. When Chris cross-examined the officer, his testimony didn't waiver one bit.

We decided earlier that I needed to take the stand because I looked like an innocent child, but I had to explain what happened to my alibi. When he asked me, what happened to my alibi, I was informed earlier by my lawyer to say that he was recovering from a motorcycle accident in San Diego.

God works in mysterious ways because the prosecutor didn't even ask to speak with Cedric via telephone, nor did he ask for a continuance to speak with him personally. God humbled him because of his arrogance and how he exalted himself.

The Judge must have thought that the police officer's testimony was enough for a conviction because the questioning ended, and the jury began their deliberations.

I was sick to my stomach and I told my mother that I had to use the bathroom. While I was in the bathroom, I heard the Holy Spirit inside of me and HE said, "The verdict was in."

For the first time in my life, I heard the audible voice of God! I left the bathroom and immediately told my mama that God had told me, "The verdict was in."

She asked, "What did God say the verdict was?"

"I don't know. He just said, 'The verdict was in.'"

Seconds later, my attorney exited the elevator and told us they had reached a decision, and we had to go back into the courtroom. I looked at Mama and said, "I told you so."

The judge asked the foreman of the jury if they had reached a decision, and he responded, "Yes, we have."

The bailiff passed the verdict to the judge and handed it back to the foreman. When he read the verdict, he said, "Not guilty!"

I had been facing a life sentence, and Jesus delivered me. I had cried out to God and He heard my cry! I broke down and cried hysterically and repeatedly said, "Thank you, Jesus! Thank you, Jesus!"

After the trial, I decided to leave Seattle and move to Parsons, Kansas.

# Chapter 16

## *Still Haven't Changed*

I should have been convicted and incarcerated in a federal penitentiary. Can you feel that? To know that you're guilty but found innocent by God's grace and favor. I felt relief knowing that it was God who delivered me despite everything I'd done. God spared my life numerous times.

This should have been enough for me to voluntarily surrender my life over to Him, but unfortunately, I still hadn't changed. These bad habits that I learned were challenging to unlearn. A part of me wanted to change, but I was fearful of the unknown. I trusted in God's words, but I still didn't completely trust God. I knew what my heart desired and it was contrary to God's words because I wanted to live according to my flesh,

I was nothing more than a lost man who loved women and money. I intentionally manipulated people to purchase more than their budget would allow.

When I visited their homes, I would have other addicts blow crack-cocaine smoke in their faces to entice them to go on a binge again. I knew if they smelled that crack smoke in the air, their addiction would overtake them. My aim was to increase their tolerance level for me to gain more revenue. The sicker they were, the more I got paid.

The more I changed, the more I hated the change. I had to come to terms with what I had done to others. I was sickened by my actions because I sold drugs to a pregnant woman who lost her child in the street. I felt compassion for what she had been through, so to help her cope with her pain from losing a child, I gave her free dope.

I sowed a lot of negativity, but I never thought what I sowed I would become. I've seen firsthand how drugs shred a family to pieces. So how was it possible for me to be the engineer behind my own demise.

I was now residing in a different city, but this time, there was a different result. The same poison that I'd been selling to others became my drug of choice: cocaine, and especially crack cocaine. When we dig a

ditch for others, we might as well dig two holes. Feel That!!

# Chapter 17

## *Worse Than Mom*

In *Feel That II: I Wish I Would Have Known,* it's a stern warning letter that tells a story of how the behavior that I hated and despised as a child became the exact behavior I emulated adult. Not only was I addicted to powder cocaine and crack cocaine; I was also addicted to pornography.

In our addition, my wife and I vowed before God never to get high without each other, and that was a lie. We vowed never to sleep around unless the other party knew prior to it, and that was a lie. And we vowed that no matter what, nothing would ever come between us or separate us from one another, and that was also a lie!

Everything that I'd achieved from selling drugs, I eventually lost—including my wife. At first, I started doing drugs recreationally, but eventually that was what I lived for. I fell asleep with it, and I woke up to it. I even had dreams about it. I carried it everywhere I would go, and if I didn't have it, my wife would do anything to get it!

Whatever you can imagine is what she would do for us to score drugs. Mom was an angel compared to what we'd done—better yet, what I allowed to be done.

I wish I had known that I was going to nearly die because of my drug usage. I wish I had known that the woman I loved would eventually divorce me and become a prostitute to support someone else's habit.

All I ever wanted to do was save one little girl from being sexually assaulted by pedophiles but now, I've destroyed thousands of lives. Is one life worth the destruction of thousands? How can one place a value on someone's life? My destruction was inevitable, but I can't forgive myself for the death and destruction of countless of lives.

I pray to God about it, but I don't get any answers. I sowed some things as a young adult and now it was time for me to enter my harvest season. Now I'd come full circle because the very thing I hated was what I'd become.

I've constantly asked myself these two questions. How did I get here and why am I still here? Hopefully, you'll never have to regretfully say, "I wish I would have known" because I'm no longer here.

It's too late for me, but maybe you want to be where I'm at. God forbids!! Because I've earned death and now, I've entered through the gate that's labeled "Welcome to Hell" where the DEAD RESIDE! *Feel That II.*

# Acknowledgements

First and foremost, I would like to thank my Lord and Savior Jesus Christ because if it wasn't for God, none of this would be possible. I would also like to give a special thank-you to my wife, S. R. James. I thank God for you, and I love you my woman of God. Everything that we have been through has been for God's glory. In that I rejoice, because of you I'm humbled.

I would also like to thank the Valdry's. I would also like to thank my mother and my sister for keeping my family held up in prayer.

B. Prose, thank you. You're someone whom I admire. Thank you for your God-sent phone call and spirit led prayer when I was about to commit suicide. You probably never knew that. When you asked me if I was alright, I said I was, but I wasn't. During that dark period of my life, I had given up on life. All glory goes to God for having you call me and stay strong in your faith in the Lord.

A special thank-you to the cover model, X. D. Finney. Joscelyn G.- - thanks for allowing Xavier to be the model for the book cover. You're truly a friend. Justin Casanova, I'm well pleased with the photography for the book cover. You did an exceptional job! Thanks.

The James' family would like to thank (from the bottom of our hearts) all those who have purchased, discussed, or even thought about purchasing our books. May our Lord and Savior Jesus Christ bless you all, and once again, thank you.

# About the Author

R. E. James is married to S. R. James. They have a total of six children, and they're currently raising their two youngest boys. R. E. James was called to be a pastor in 2010, and he ran from his calling for many years. He's pursuing his master's degree in Christian Ministry, and his wife is a pursuing her master's as a Nurse Practitioner. They put God first in every aspect of their lives, and they have learned the hard way not to lean on their own understanding. Their hope is always in the Lord and that HOPE does NOT disappoint.

## FeelThat Trilogy

Feel That               Feel That II               Felt That

## The Simplys Collection

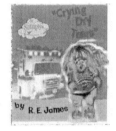

# The Simplys Collection

1.  Don't Want to Be Me.

2.  The Simplys "We are Simply Who We Are"

3.  The Simplys "It's Okay to Say I'm Not Okay"

4.  The Simplys "Crying Dry Tears"

    The Simplys "Crying Dry Tears II"

5.  The Simplys "Pick your Battles Don't let Your Battles Pick You"

6.  The Simplys "Blurred Vision with Clear Thoughts"

7.  The Simplys "The Designer and The Manufacturer"

8.  The Simplys "Who you Choose to follow determines Where You Will Go"

9.  The Simplys "Going to School on an Empty Stomach"

88742038R00109

Made in the USA
San Bernardino, CA
15 September 2018